"Written by a dramatist of ambitious scope and fierce focus, *Sweat* is a bracingly topical portrait of American dreams deferred. It warrants serious applause."

—BEN BRANTLEY, *NEW YORK TIMES*

"A powerful and compassionate song of blue-collar despair."

—DAVID ROONEY, *HOLLYWOOD REPORTER*

"Where can we turn for enlightenment now that the toxic Political Super Bowl is over? Is there anyone to lead us from the simplistic sound bites that have relegated us into enemy camps? Enter Lynn Nottage, a distinguished American playwright who set out to better understand the anger of today's betrayed working class . . . *Sweat* roils with anger and frustration, but these feelings are put in the service of a public good: fostering solidarity where polarization has grown most extreme . . . *Sweat* offers a path toward healing for a nation riven by a torturous election. We would all be well served to follow Nottage's compassionately wise example and venture outside our comfort zones and unplug our ears."

—CHARLES MCNULTY, *LOS ANGELES TIMES*

"*Sweat* is a play that will be performed long after the era it defines has passed." —ROBERT HOFLER, *WRAP*

"An excellent and highly charged play . . . It is refreshing to hear characters talk about politics as urgently, and realistically, as people are affected by it. *Sweat* is politics as lived and spoken about on the ground, not as an abstraction, and not as a Washington power-game, or a shrieking panel on CNN. *Sweat* explains the gestation of discontent, mixed with racism and fears over immigration, that led to many perhaps casting their vote for Trump."

—TIM TEEMAN, *DAILY BEAST*

"A brilliant play . . . No play in recent memory has shed more light on the crises and tribulations of America's great retrenched working middle class . . . Nottage writes fully realized characters who, especially when acting on their worst fears, are grippingly human . . . *Sweat* never feels less than authentic—and crucial."

—JEREMY GERARD, *DEADLINE*

SWEAT

SWEAT

LYNN NOTTAGE

THEATRE COMMUNICATIONS GROUP   NEW YORK   2017

"Let America Be America Again," by Langston Hughes, written in 1935, copyright © 1994 by the Estate of Langston Hughes, from *The Collected Poems of Langston Hughes*, Alfred A. Knopf, Inc., New York.

The publication of *Sweat* by Lynn Nottage, through TCG's Book Program, is made possible in part by the New York State Council on the Arts with the support of Governor Andrew Cuomo and the New York State Legislature.

Special thanks to Paula Marie Black for her generous support of this publication.

TCG books are exclusively distributed to the book trade by Consortium Book Sales and Distribution.

Library of Congress Control Numbers:
2017000957 (print) / 2017006056 (ebook)
ISBN 978-1-55936-532-1 (softcover) / ISBN 978-1-55936-854-4 (ebook)
A catalog record for this book is available from the Library of Congress.

Book design and composition by Lisa Govan
Cover design by Mark Melnick
Cover photographs by Henry Sene Yee

First Edition, May 2017
Third Printing, September 2017

For Wallace Nottage

SPECIAL THANKS TO:

Bill Rauch, Alison Carey, Julie Felise Dubiner, Molly Smith, Oskar Eustis, Mandy Hackett, Maria Goyanes, Mica Cole, and Robert Barry Fleming.

Stuart Thompson and Louise L. Gund.

John Eisner, Arthur Kopit, The Lark, Christopher Oscar Peña, Kimber Lee, Rogelio Martinez, Gus Schulenburg, Emily Mann, The McCarter Theatre, and Kevin Emrick.

A heartfelt thanks to Travis Ballenger, Kate Whoriskey, Tony Gerber, Santo D. Marabella, Olivier Sultan, Pat Giles, William Davis, Doug Graybill, Dean Showers, United Steel Workers— Local 6996, Phillip Howze, Ruby Aiyo Gerber, Melkamu Gerber, Todd Leatherman, Erin Washington, Amber Espinosa-Jones, Violet Overn, and the people of Reading who opened up their lives to me.

And my gratitude to the spectacular cast, designers, and crew at Oregon Shakespeare Festival; Arena Stage; The Public Theater; and Studio 54, Broadway.

In memory of Ruth M. Mathews.

PRODUCTION HISTORY

Sweat was co-commissioned by the Oregon Shakespeare Festival (Bill Rauch, Artistic Director; Cynthia Rider, Executive Director) through its American Revolutions: The United States History Cycle and the Arena Stage (Molly Smith, Artistic Director; Edgar Dobie, Executive Producer), and received its world premiere at the Oregon Shakespeare Festival in Ashland, Oregon, on July 29, 2015. The production was directed by Kate Whoriskey. The set design was by John Lee Beatty, the costume design was by Jennifer Moeller, the lighting design was by Peter Kaczorowski, the sound design was by Michael Bodeen and Rob Milburn, the video design was by Jeff Sugg, the fight direction was by U. Jonathan Toppo, and the dramaturgy was by Julie Felise Dubiner; the production stage manager was Jill Rendall. The cast was:

EVAN	Tyrone Wilson
JASON	Stephen Michael Spencer
CHRIS	Tramell Tillman
STAN	Jack Willis
OSCAR	Carlo Albán
TRACEY	Terri McMahon
CYNTHIA	Kimberly Scott
JESSIE	K. T. Vogt
BRUCIE	Kevin Kenerly

The production opened at the Arena Stage in Washington, D.C. on January 15, 2016. All personnel remained the same with the following exceptions: the production stage manager was Kurt Hall. The cast was:

EVAN	Tyrone Wilson
JASON	Stephen Michael Spencer
CHRIS	Tramell Tillman
STAN	Jack Willis
OSCAR	Reza Salazar
TRACEY	Johanna Day
CYNTHIA	Kimberly Scott
JESSIE	Tara Mallen
BRUCIE	Kevin Kenerly

Sweat received its New York premiere at the Public Theater (Oskar Eustis, Artistic Director; Patrick Willingham, Executive Director) on November 3, 2016. The production was directed by Kate Whoriskey. The set design was by John Lee Beatty, the costume design was by Jennifer Moeller, the lighting design was by Peter Kaczorowski, the sound design was by Michael Bodeen and Rob Milburn, the video design was by Jeff Sugg, the fight direction was by U. Jonathan Toppo, hair and makeup design were by Leah J. Loukas; the production stage manager was Donald Fried, and the stage manager was Alexandra Hall. The cast was:

EVAN	Lance Coadie Williams
JASON	Will Pullen
CHRIS	Khris Davis
STAN	James Colby
OSCAR	Carlo Albán
TRACEY	Johanna Day
CYNTHIA	Michelle Wilson
JESSIE	Miriam Shor
BRUCIE	John Earl Jelks

The production received its Broadway premiere on March 26, 2017 at Studio 54. It was produced by Stuart Thompson and Louise L. Gund. The co-producers were Tulchin Bartner Productions, Jon B. Platt, Roy Furman, Len Blavatnik, Shelly Mitchell, Scott Rudin, Ted Snowdon, Kevin Emrick, True Love Productions, John Gore, Deborah Taylor/Richard Winkler, and The Public Theater. The personnel and cast remained the same with the following exception:

JESSIE   Alison Wright

CHARACTERS

EVAN, African-American, forties

JASON, white American of German descent, twenty-one/twenty-nine

CHRIS, African-American, twenty-one/twenty-nine

STAN, white American of German descent, fifties

OSCAR, Colombian-American, twenty-two/thirty

TRACEY, white American of German descent, forty-five/fifty-three

CYNTHIA, African-American, forty-five/fifty-three

JESSIE, Italian-American, forties

BRUCIE, African-American, forties

All of the characters were born in Berks County, Pennsylvania.

SWEAT

O, yes,
I say it plain,
America never was America to me,
And yet I swear this oath—
America will be!

Out of the rack and ruin of our gangster death,
The rape and rot of graft, and stealth, and lies,
We, the people, must redeem
The land, the mines, the plants, the rivers.
The mountains and the endless plain—
All, all the stretch of these great green states—
And make America again!

—Langston Hughes

ACT ONE

SCENE 1

September 29, 2008

Outside it's 72°F.
In the news: The 63rd session of the United Nations General Assembly convenes. The Dow Jones Industrial Average falls 778.68 points, marking the largest single-day decline in stock market history. Reading residents sample fresh apple cider at the Annual Fall Festival on Old Dry Road Farm.
Music. Lights up.
Parole office. Spare. Institutional.
Jason (white American, twenty-nine), hair closely shorn. He has a black eye and white supremacist tattoos inked across his face. Evan (African-American, forties), comfortably puffy.

EVAN: So, you got a job?
JASON: Yeah.
EVAN: I'm not gonna run down everything. You know the drill.

JASON: Yeah.

EVAN: So, you're making pretzels?

JASON: Yeah.

(A moment.)

EVAN: Soft?

JASON: Yeah.

EVAN: Living at the same address?

JASON: Yeah.

EVAN: The mission?

JASON: Yeah, finally got a bed downstairs.

EVAN: That's real good. I hear that shelter's pretty clean.

JASON: Yeah, but fucking guys steal. Can't have nice stuff. But, um, Father Hunt lets me keep my turtles.

(Jason fidgets. Evan assesses.)

EVAN: So. You gonna tell me what happened?

JASON: What?

EVAN: I know you don't wanna be here. I don't wanna be here either.

JASON: Yeah, whatever.

EVAN: Don't whatever me. I'm not one of your stupid friends, let's be clear about that.

JASON: Whatever.

EVAN: Try me! I'm not playing fucking games. I'll knock you clear into tomorrow, understood? But, fortunately for you, I don't have to, you know why? Because I got this pen, and you know what this pen does?

JASON: Yeah—

EVAN: It writes. And, you know what it's gonna write if you don't give me more than one- or two-syllable answers? It's gonna write that you're belligerent, defiant, reluctant to observe protocol. You understand those words, Jason?

JASON: Yeah.

EVAN (*Voice slowly crescendos*): It's gonna write that you have issues with authority that may prove too challenging. This pen could make things very difficult for you, young man. And you know what happens to young men that don't cooperate? . . . Huh? . . . Huh?

JASON: You asking me?

EVAN: Whatcha think I'm asking—myself? Of course I'm asking you, moron! You want me to ask again?

JASON: No. I don't need you to ask again.

EVAN: Very good. A sentence. We're making some progress here. So, what happened?

JASON: I mean . . . I didn't do shit.

EVAN: So you didn't do shit, but someone did . . . do shit.

JASON: Uh—

EVAN: And, you gave yourself a black eye and busted lip?

(*A moment.*)

What happened?

JASON: I got sucker-punched.

EVAN: Cuz—?

JASON: I dunno.

EVAN: Some guy just comes up and hits ya. And you, you didn't do nothing?

JASON: Nah. Not really. I was in the bathroom at Loco's.

EVAN: Loco's?

JASON: Yeah, Loco's.

EVAN: I'm sorry? Loco's?

JASON: I can't go to Loco's?

EVAN: We've talked about Loco's. Go on.

JASON: This big fucking biker dude, I don't know 'em, like steps up behind me. He's like you were looking at my girl. I am so, like, dude, I don't even know who the fuck your girl is. And he's wearing these huge rings, both fucking hands, like medieval biker knight.

EVAN: Hmm.

JASON: And . . . then he hits me hard, so hard that I swear to God I see stars. Like Bam! My whole face goes numb. Sparky had to pull 'em off of me.

EVAN: Just because you looked at his girl.

JASON: I didn't look at his girl, that's why it's so fucked up.

EVAN: And if I ask you to piss in this cup, what's it gonna tell me?

JASON: You don't gotta believe me, but I'm telling ya the // truth.

EVAN: Okay. There's the cup.

JASON: What?

EVAN: What do you mean, what?

JASON: C'mon.

EVAN: The cup, pick it up.

JASON: I just got a job. What do you want?

EVAN: I don't want anything from you, but the state does and it's my unfortunate job to ensure that you comply.

JASON: Are we gonna do this?

EVAN: Pick it up.

JASON: You are a fucking asshole. Fuck you, nigga!

(A moment. Evan, stone, stares long and hard at Jason.)

(Less committed) Fuck you!

EVAN: Pick it up!

JASON: I got a job. I mean, c'mon, give me a fucking break.

EVAN: Pick . . . it . . . up!

(Jason makes a show of picking up the cup.)

Okay. What do you wanna tell me?

(A moment.)

JASON: I dunno.

EVAN: I dunno, either.

JASON: Look—

EVAN: What?

JASON: I dunno.

EVAN: Yeah, we covered that fertile territory. What's going on Jason?

JASON: Yo, ease up. I'm doing what I am supposed to be doing.

EVAN: You think so? You looking to get back inside?

JASON: . . . !

EVAN: Might wanna get rid of those tats. We've talked about it. They're gonna cause you trouble out here. Might make you a tough guy inside, out here . . . guess what? Every time I look at them I wanna punch you out. That's me being honest. But, lucky for you I'm here to help.

(Jason fidgets.)

What's going on Jason? I shouldn't have to track you down.

(A moment. Jason rolls his eyes.)

JASON: Can I go?

EVAN: We don't have to talk. It's no sweat off my back. I'm gonna leave this page blank. How about that? Blank page. You wanna blank page?

JASON: . . .

EVAN: You in trouble?

JASON: No.

EVAN: I could fish all day. I am a fisherman.

(Jason runs a story through his head, deciding whether to share it.)

JASON: I—

EVAN: Yeah—

JASON: Ran into Chris.

(Jason is caught off-guard by his own emotions.)

EVAN: All right? You okay? We knew this might happen. Yeah?

JASON: Yeah.

EVAN: He's out there. He ain't going nowhere. Whatcha gonna do about it?

JASON: I dunno. I dunno. The whole time inside, I pushed what happened, you know, Chris, all of it, outta my head. Then he was . . . I dunno, it's all I can think, you know—

(Evan turns around, and he's now talking to Chris [African-American, twenty-nine]. He is very neatly dressed, but quite fidgety and anxious.)

EVAN: You okay, man? You seem antsy.

CHRIS: Not gonna lie, it's been tough. Not sleeping so good. Still trying to get used to things.

EVAN: Well, you been away a long time. The river keeps flowing.

CHRIS *(Anxious)*: I guess. People. Psh. People, they're a trip. You know? Before it was . . . um . . . it was easy, now every conversation I have, it's like I'm circling in a traffic pattern, just circling. I don't got shit to say to anyone, and nobody got shit to say to me.

EVAN: You find someplace to stay . . . Chris?

CHRIS: Yeah. Reverend Duckett lets me sleep in the rectory. I do some chores. It's all right for now. Quiet. Trying to find my feet.

EVAN: It's gonna be that way for a while.

CHRIS: Yeah, I'm figuring that out quickly!

EVAN: What about work?

CHRIS: Looking.

EVAN: Did you follow up with the leads I gave you?

CHRIS: Yeah, went down there, filled out a few applications, but they ain't offering nothing real, I'm talking bullshit, you know . . . seven, eight dollars an hour.

EVAN: Gotta begin somewhere.

CHRIS: I guess. And I keep hitting up against that box. That damn question's a barbed-wire fence, can't go over it, can't get around it.

EVAN: I know, I know. But, whatcha doing to keep your head?

CHRIS: Going to prayer meetings. Doing it one day at a time. Reverend Duckett has been real cool to me.

EVAN: Good. Good. What about that prison program? How many credits you short?

CHRIS: Eight. But first . . . I gotta throw a little money in my pocket. Get things on track, you know. Then, psh, I can think about finishing up my bachelor's.

EVAN: I'm really glad to hear that.

CHRIS: That was the plan, you know, before the shit went down.

EVAN: You seem a little on edge today.

CHRIS: Yeah, well. Some days are like that. I get real mad at myself.

(A moment. Chris, suddenly introspective.)

EVAN: You okay? You need some air or something?

CHRIS: Nah. I . . . I ran into Jason. Wasn't expecting it.

EVAN: What was that like?

CHRIS: Weird . . . weird. He looked different.

EVAN: Yeah?

CHRIS: He had tats on his face. Big fucking tats. He looked ridiculous. I had to deal with that bullshit inside. You know, Aryan Brotherhood. But, Jason . . . that shit surprised me. He looked old, like a man. Like his dad useta, before he died. It kinda freaked me out.

EVAN: I bet.

CHRIS *(Escalating emotions)*: I dunno. A couple minutes, and your whole life changes, that's it. It's gone. Every day I think about what if I hadn't . . . You know . . . I run it and run it, a tape over and over again. What if. What if. What if. All night. In my head. I can't turn it off. Reverend Duckett said, "Lean on God for forgiveness. Lean on God to find your way through the terrible storm." I'm leaning into the wind, I'm fuckin' leaning . . . And.

(A moment.)

And then there's Jason. Crossing Penn, you know, and I'm just chilling, looking in the window of Sneaker Villa, not thinking about anything. He sees me. I see him. Neither of us could . . . um, move for a second. We . . . it was . . . I've been thinking about what I would do in that moment. How I would react, what I would say. I mean . . . fuck it. What we did was unforgivable . . .

EVAN: So, what—?

CHRIS: Next thing I know I'm walking fast toward him, I don't know what I'm gonna do. But the emotions are right there in my chest. A fist pressing right there. Pressing. And I keep walking. And I'm expecting him to walk away, do something, but he just stands there like he's been waiting on me all these years. And . . . we come face to face. Like right there. I can smell his breath, that's how close we are. I can see the fucking veins in his eyes. And my fists clench. My fingernails dig into the palms of my hands and then it just happens . . . weird . . . We're hugging. Hugging. I don't know why. And for the first time in eight years, I feel like I could go home.

(Tears are close, but they don't come.

A loud blast of music: Santana's "Smooth." The past rips through 2008.)

SCENE 2

January 18, 2000

Eight years earlier.
Outside it's 19°F.
In the news: American think tanks report that the booming stock market is widening the income gap between the poorest and richest U.S. families. Reading passes an aggressive dog ordinance to regulate ownership of certain pet breeds including pit bulls.
Santana's "Smooth" plays loudly from a jukebox.
Lights up. Bar. Lived-in and comfortable. End of a raucous celebration. Music blares.
Cynthia (African-American, forty-five) and Tracey (white American, forty-five), just a little too drunk, are dancing. Stan (white American, fifties), the bartender, stands behind the bar, smiling, and enjoying the show. Jessie (Italian-American, forties) is passed out, face planted on the table.

Tracey and Cynthia dance together with the intimacy of close friends who've shared many adventures.

CYNTHIA: C'mon, Stan.

STAN: Nah, don't dance!

CYNTHIA: I don't believe ya!

TRACEY: Stan the man! Don't fail me! I know ya got some moves!

STAN: Nope!

(Tracey does a sexy, enticing dance.)

Don't break anything.

(The music ends.)

CYNTHIA AND TRACEY: Aww.

(Cynthia walks over to the jukebox. Tracey flops down next to Jessie and finishes her friend's drink.)

STAN: Hey. Who's driving her home?

TRACEY: Howard just locks up and leaves her there. Somehow she always manages to punch in to work on time. Right, Cynth?

CYNTHIA: Showered and dressed.

TRACEY: We all got a seven A.M. call and that one's out drinking until two every night.

STAN: Well, someone's gotta drive her.

TRACEY: Not happening. I got the inside of my car cleaned Thursday.

STAN: Hey, Cynthia, can you drive Jessie home?

CYNTHIA: Hell no, she was the designated driver.

(Tracey laughs and nudges Jessie.)

TRACEY: Jessie!

(Jessie rouses.)

JESSIE: What?!

(She slumps back onto the table. Laughter.)

STAN: Well, she can't stay here.

(Stan, with a pronounced limp, an old bothersome injury, hobbles over, and takes Jessie's keys from her pocket. He throws them into a key jar on the shelf.)

CYNTHIA: How many keys you collect?
STAN: Didn't fill the jar, but the night's still young.

(Stan places a bottle of bourbon on the bar.)

One more drink?

(He pours Tracey a drink.)

TRACEY: Now, you're really trying to get over.
STAN *(Seductively)*: It's an open invitation.
TRACEY: Yeah? Really?

(Stan gives her a disarmingly seductive smile and strokes her arm.)

Nice. Does that work for you? Because, I'm not feeling anything. I mean should I be feeling something?
STAN: I'm definitely reading something.
TRACEY: Get outta here! It was one fucking time, it's definitely not happening again.

(Stan continues to work his charm.)

STAN: Two.

TRACEY: Not technically.

STAN: Oh really?

TRACEY: Really!

(Tracey laughs. She's a laugher, it's her refuge.
Oscar, the Colombian-American busboy, twenty-two, hauls in
a rack of glasses. He wipes down the bar. He goes about his busi-
ness, rarely acknowledged by anyone except Stan.)

STAN: Thanks, Oscar.

CYNTHIA: Okay. I love you, but I'm officially drunk-b-dunk, which means I gotta go.

TRACEY: No . . .

CYNTHIA: Got an early shift.

TRACEY: Frank can kiss my ass. Jesus, haven't you done enough overtime?

CYNTHIA: Babe, come hell or high water, I'm taking that cruise through the Panama Canal this summer.

TRACEY: One more drink. One. It's my birthday. C'mon, c'mon. Stan, pour this bitch another drink!

CYNTHIA: Okay. But, if I lose a finger in the mill, it'll be your fault. Remember that. It's her fault!

STAN: It's her fault!

(Tracey gives Cynthia a hug. Stan chuckles and pours Cynthia's
drink.)

CYNTHIA: You gonna have a drink with us?

TRACEY: One . . .

STAN: Sure. Two pretty ladies. No downside to that.

TRACEY: Watch what he's putting in there. That's how I got into trouble last time.

STAN *(Seductively)*: Oh, c'mon, trouble?

What a night! A lot of folks turned out to celebrate.

TRACEY: It was fun, huh? Never thought I'd make it to this age.

STAN: Tell me about it. Hadn't seen some of those guys in ages. And I was kinda hopin' I'd see Brucie.

(A moment. Tracey looks at Cynthia.)

CYNTHIA: Well, don't hold your breath. I put his ass out.

STAN: Oh no. What happened?

CYNTHIA: I let him move back in.

TRACEY: // Told ya.

CYNTHIA: You know Brucie, he can be as smooth as satin. Turn that shit on and off at the drop of a dime. Things were going fine, then Christmas Day, we've got this nice bottle of Chablis. He's looking dapper. I'm dressed for danger. We're laughing, chilling and having fun. And . . . we talk. I mean, talk. It's all good. We drink wine, we drink some more wine, then we do what you do after you drink too much wine. Middle of the night—

TRACEY: Listen to this—

CYNTHIA: I go downstairs. My Christmas presents under the tree are gone—

STAN: // Get outta here.

CYNTHIA: AND my fish tank with my expensive new tropical fish, gone.

STAN: Don't tell me—

CYNTHIA: A week later, New Year's Eve, I wake up. And this fool's digging in the refrigerator like he actually put something there. High as a muthafucking kite. Says nothing. No apology. Nada. I damn near lost my mind. Brucie was lucky I wasn't holding a gun, cuz right now he'd be in hell trying to hustle the devil.

STAN: That don't sound like him.

CYNTHIA: The hell it don't, let me tell you something, once he started messing with that dope, I don't recognize the man. I know it's tough out there, I understand. Yeah, yeah,

yeah. He went through hell when his plant locked him out, I understand, but I can't have it.

TRACEY: More importantly, you don't // have to.

STAN: So, what—?

CYNTHIA: I tell that joker, it's time to go. Bye-bye. And we get into it. Police come down, chest-pumped, I get cuffed, photographed and fingerprinted for disorderly conduct in my own damn house.

STAN: No way.

CYNTHIA: Yes . . .	TRACEY: Yeah, can you believe it? I had to go down there and bail her out. New Year's Eve. I'm wearing heels and a sequin dress.

STAN: Jesus. What about Brucie?

CYNTHIA: Ask me if I give a goddamn.

STAN: Tough. Sorry to hear it. You two were good together.

CYNTHIA: Yeah, well, not anymore.

STAN: Oh shit, speaking of arrests, did you guys read about Freddy in the paper this morning?

CYNTHIA: No, what was Freddy doing in the paper?

STAN: God, you didn't hear?

TRACEY: Nah. What happened?

STAN: He burned his fucking house down.

CYNTHIA: What?

TRACEY: Was anybody hurt?

STAN: Just the dog.

CYNTHIA: Pepper? Oh my God—

STAN: Yeah, crazy, huh?

CYNTHIA: Oh my // God

TRACEY: What about Maggie?

STAN: I thought you knew, she walked out . . . two weeks ago.

CYNTHIA: What?	TRACEY: What happened?

STAN: Yeah.

(Jessie rouses for a second.)

STAN: Gone.   JESSIE: Yeah!

CYNTHIA: That's some shit.
TRACEY: Our Freddy? Freddy Brunner?
STAN: Freddy—
CYNTHIA: I don't get it. Why would the man burn down his own house?

STAN: // Dunno.   TRACEY: Crazy.
   Three-alarm fire.   That sucks.
   Nothing // left.

STAN: He was in here on Saturday, got shit-faced. Maggie just up and left him—
TRACEY: Where would that bitch go?
STAN: That's what he said. Dunno. The paper says he tried to shoot himself in the head. Can you believe it? But, he was too wasted, and ended up shooting off his right ear.

TRACEY: Ow.   CYNTHIA: Get the hell outta here.

STAN: They found him lying on his neighbor's lawn, bleeding—
CYNTHIA: Damn. That's all I gotta say. // DAMN!
TRACEY: Freddy Brunner?
STAN: Turns out he was up to his neck in fucking debt.
TRACEY: Terrible—
STAN: And Clarence—
CYNTHIA: Clarence Jones?
STAN: Says he got wind that they were gonna cut back his line at the plant. Couldn't handle the stress.
CYNTHIA: That rumor's been flying around for months. Nobody's going anywhere.

SWEAT

STAN: Okay, you keep telling yourself that, but you saw what happened over at Clemmons Technologies. No one saw that coming. Right? You could wake up tomorrow and all your jobs are in Mexico, whatever, it's this NAFTA bullshit—

TRACEY: What the fuck is NAFTA? Sounds like a laxative. NAFTA.

(Tracey laughs.)

STAN: You don't read the paper?

TRACEY: You read the paper?

STAN: Yes, I do.

TRACEY: Well, I don't read the paper, okay? I'm dyslexic, thank you.

STAN: Eyes open. Not a good philosophy to resist knowledge.

TRACEY: Where'd you read that bullshit?

STAN: I didn't read it, I intuit it.

CYNTHIA: Whatever. It's a rumor. Management // spreads that crap to keep us on edge.

STAN: I'm just saying. But, it ain't my problem // anymore.

TRACEY: Hey, is it against the law to burn down your own house?

STAN: Dunno. I think you need a permit.

(Jessie rouses again.)

JESSIE: Where's the FIRE at?   TRACEY: What?!

STAN: A permit.

TRACEY: Really? For your own damn house?

STAN: Ya can't set a fire that big without a permit.

TRACEY: Wait a minute, you're saying if he got a permit he could legally burn his house down?

JESSIE: Yeah.

CYNTHIA: Shit, I should burn down my house. Crappy little money trap.

TRACEY: To hell with the permit, I'd hire someone else to do it.

CYNTHIA: Shut up, who do you know?

TRACEY: I dunno.

(Tracey laughs, then gestures to Oscar.)

Hey. What about you?

OSCAR: Me? What? Ya need water?

TRACEY: No, but . . . if I wanted to hire someone to burn down my house where would I go?

OSCAR: I dunno. How would I know?

TRACEY: What do you mean, you don't know? C'mon.

OSCAR: I don't know.

TRACEY: You Puerto Ricans are burning shit down all over Reading, you gotta know.

OSCAR: Well, I'm Colombian. And I don't know.

TRACEY: Yeah, right.

CYNTHIA: Ignore her. She's stupid.

TRACEY: He fucking knows, he's just not saying.

CYNTHIA: Let it go!

TRACEY: He fucking knows.

STAN: Lighten up! Let it go!

OSCAR: Psh.

TRACEY: Psh.

(Oscar cuts his eyes at Tracey and walks back to the bar. Stan redirects Tracey, defusing the tension.)

STAN: Hey, you know, Freddy was on the line with my old man. He trained me. Yeah.

CYNTHIA: Really?

STAN: As matter of fact, when I got injured, it was Freddy who shut down the mill.

TRACEY: I didn't know that.

STAN: Yeah. If it wasn't for him. I would have lost my entire leg.

(Jessie suddenly alert:)

JESSIE: Hey, Stan, quit yapping, get me another gimlet.

STAN: You're joking. Absolutely not.

JESSIE: What? Are you the bartender on tonight?

STAN: Not giving you another drink.

JESSIE: C'mon! Gimme another drink! You gave her a drink, why can't I have one?

STAN: Because that's how it goes. You've had enough.

JESSIE: You got a fucking problem.

STAN: No, you got a fucking problem.

JESSIE: You can't talk to me that way. My husband—

STAN: You mean your ex.

JESSIE: All I gotta do is make one phone call and he'll wipe that fucking smile off your face.

STAN: Yeah, go ahead. Here, use my phone. Wake up his beautiful young wife, what's her name again, Tiffany?

CYNTHIA: That wasn't // necessary.

JESSIE: You are a asshole!

STAN: Take her home.

TRACEY: C'mon. // Don't start this again—

JESSIE: You fucking cripple.

STAN: Nice language.	CYNTHIA: She's had a little too much to drink.

STAN: And that's why it's time for her to go home. Night-night.

JESSIE: I'll kick your ass, gimp!

(*Jessie struggles to her feet. She attempts to walk, but is completely wasted.*)

CYNTHIA: Jessie. // C'mon.

JESSIE: Cripple! You fucking warlock!

CYNTHIA: Calm down.	STAN: Relax . . .

CYNTHIA: All right. We're celebrating . . .

JESSIE: Fucker. Fucker!!   STAN: That's nice . . . Nice . .

CYNTHIA: You've had enough. Okay. Calm the fuck down.
JESSIE *(Snaps)*: Don't talk to me!
CYNTHIA: Don't start with me, babe.

(Cynthia makes an "I mean business" face. Tracey laughs.)

JESSIE: Oh shit.
CYNTHIA: You okay? You need a hand?

(Jessie struggles to walk to the bathroom, attempting to maintain her dignity, but it's a herculean task. Finally:)

STAN: Hey Oscar, give her a hand.
OSCAR: Okay.

(Jessie leans onto Oscar.)

Hold onto me. I gotchu.
JESSIE: Are we together?
OSCAR: No!
CYNTHIA: And get her a glass of water.
TRACEY: You mean a gallon.

(Oscar leads Jessie to the bathroom.)

OSCAR: Just a couple of steps. Okay. Take your time.
STAN: Jesus. Fucking pathetic.
CYNTHIA *(To Tracey)*: I thought you were gonna talk to her! She
    keeps showing up at work smelling like a bottle of vodka.
TRACEY: No shit, she's been a complete wreck since Dan got
    remarried.
CYNTHIA: // Talk to her!
TRACEY: My husband died and you don't see me bathing in
    booze. And I'm sorry, but I just can't hear her go on about

him one more time. He was a creep, and it's my fucking birthday, you'd think she'd be able to hold it together.

CYNTHIA: I know, but seriously, talk to her. Someone's gonna get hurt.

TRACEY: You gonna report her?

CYNTHIA: Listen babe, they're always looking for reasons to let us go. 'Specially now, with this damn shake up—

STAN: Then the rumor's true, huh? Butz is getting promoted?

CYNTHIA: Yeah.

TRACEY: He's heading to some plant outta state.

STAN: Who they bringing in?

TRACEY: They're talking about hiring someone from the floor.

STAN: Get outta here. Really? You gonna apply?

TRACEY: Me? No fucking way.

(Stan glances over at Cynthia.)

STAN: You're awful quiet, Cynth.

CYNTHIA: Who knows? I might apply.

TRACEY: What?! Get outta here.

CYNTHIA: Why the hell not? I've got twenty-four years on the floor.

TRACEY: Well, I got you beat by two. Started in '74, walked in straight outta high school. First and only job. Management is for them. Not us.

CYNTHIA: More money. More heat. More vacation. Less work. That's all I need to know.

TRACEY: Hey Stan, how many years did you put in before the injury?

STAN: Twenty-eight.

TRACEY: And in those twenty-eight years you ever see anyone move off the floor?

STAN: . . . Um, no . . . wait, wait . . . there was Griff Parker.

TRACEY: Yeah, but he left, went to college came back as management. They didn't pluck him off the line. Doesn't count.

CYNTHIA: Shit, you wanna be fifty and standing on your feet f
ten hours a day? Titties sagging into the machines. I got
bunions the size of damn apples. // My back—

TRACEY: Bla . . . bla. Write a book.

CYNTHIA: Don't know about you, but I can feel my body slow-
ing down, a little every day. I go home and my hands are
frozen, I can't even hold a frying pan. I gotta rub 'em
together for an hour before they even move.

TRACEY: But be serious, Butz's job?

CYNTHIA: I know the machines. I know the people.

TRACEY: Hold on, hold on. You're really gonna apply?! No
bullshit.

CYNTHIA: All they can do is say no, right Stan?

STAN: That's right.

(A moment.)

TRACEY: Well . . . If that's the case, maybe I should throw my
name into the mix. Right? I need a vacation. I got the same
experience you got. But, I mean none of us girls are gonna
get it, right?

CYNTHIA: It's been a helluva lot better since Olstead's grandson
took over—

STAN: Gimme a break. That place hasn't changed since I walked
in there in '69. Not a lightbulb, not one single nut or bolt.
As a matter of fact it hasn't changed much since my grandfather began working there in '22. Good luck, sweetheart.
I don't know him, but I can tell you that Olstead's grandson
is the same brand of asshole as all of 'em, stuffing his pockets, rather than improving the floor.

CYNTHIA: // Word.

STAN: Now, the old man, he used to be on the floor every single
day. I didn't like him, but I respected him for it. You know
why?

TRACEY: He was a prick and a perv—

STAN: Because he knew what was going on, and you can only know that by being there. A machine was broken, he knew. A worker was having trouble, he knew. You don't see the young guys out there. They find it offensive to be on the floor with their Wharton MBAs. And the problem is they don't wanna get their feet dirty, their diplomas soiled with sweat . . . or understand the real cost, the human cost of making their shitty product.

CYNTHIA: Amen to that.

JESSIE *(From off)*: Oh, shit.

(From off, a crash and a thud.)

STAN: Hey, maybe one of you should check on Jessie.

TRACEY: Nah, she's fine.

CYNTHIA: Did you get a load of what she's wearing? Looks like her prom dress.

TRACEY: Probably was.

(Jessie reenters unseen. Her dress is caught up in the back of her underwear.)

CYNTHIA: I love that woman, but she's gonna drag us all down with her.

JESSIE: Who?

CYNTHIA: Don't worry about it, babe.

JESSIE: Were you talking about me?

CYNTHIA: We're just talking.

JESSIE: Okay.

(A moment.)

Stan, can I get another gim—

STAN: No! N-O.

JESSIE: You're bullshit.

STAN: I can live with that.

JESSIE: Bullshit!

STAN: Enough already. Jesus.

TRACEY: C'mon, Jessie, relax.

CYNTHIA: Get your shit together. Frank's lookii

TRACEY: Can we not have this conversation, it̮ ᵁᵁᵁ cutting into my buzz. We've been having the same conversation for twenty years. So, let's stop complaining and have some fun.

(Music. Laughter. Celebration.)

SCENE 3

February 10, 2000

Outside it's 44°F.

In the news: Billionaire Steve Forbes drops out of the Republican Primary after investing $66,000,000 of his own money. Work begins on the Downtown Civic Convention Center in Reading.

Lights up. Bar. Chris and Jason, their younger selves, stand at the bar, tipsy. Once again, Oscar is a quiet but visible presence throughout the scene, watching, listening and working.

JASON: I spoke to the owner. It has something like twenty-three-thousand miles on it. Can you believe it? An old man kept it in his garage like a trophy. It's in beautiful condition. Mint.

CHRIS: Phat. You gonna do it?

JASON: Thinking about it.

CHRIS: Dude.

(Jason proudly displays a picture.)

JASON: What do you think?

STAN: Nice.

JASON: Right. It's exactly like the one my dad had, but in better condition. Yo, check out the logo on the side. Dooope . . .

STAN: A Harley? What's your mom think?

JASON: So as far as I'm concerned, if she ain't paying for it then she don't got no say. In October, when I turned twenty-one, she made it dead clear that her work was done. She changed the locks on the front door and didn't give me a key. That sends a pretty clear fucking message, huh?

CHRIS: Yo.

STAN: That kinda sounds like Tracey.

JASON: All I can say is that when I saw the bike, my first urge was to fuck it.

(Jason simulates humping the bike.)

CHRIS: Get outta here.

(Throughout the scene, Oscar scraps gum from the bottom of the tables. It is an unpleasant task, but Oscar is focused and determined.)

STAN: Yeah? Whatcha waiting on, why don't you buy it?

JASON: I figure I got another *(Calculating)* month and half of saving and it's mine. Fucking union got all our money tied up in benefits and shit, don't have nothing left for fun.

CHRIS: You ain't lying. Between my new lady—

JASON: Monique!

CHRIS: —and Uncle Sam, money got a way of running outcha pocket. Nobody tells you that no matter how hard you work there will never be enough money to rest. It's fact. A fact that should be taught to every child! Look at me. I been trying to save a little something for school, right?

But every time I tuck it away, I hear the cry of "Nike Flightposite," "Air Jordan XV," a meal at the Olive Garden, and a movie will set you back two days' work.

JASON: Dude, you got more sneakers than the entire Sixers.

CHRIS: No swagger without the proper kicks. It's how I roll. A man gotta have one vice that keeps him hungry.

STAN: Is that a rule?

CHRIS: No, no my friend it's a mandate.

JASON: And, wait a minute, did I . . . did I hear you say school?

CHRIS: Yeah. School. S-C-H-O-O-L!

JASON: Thanks for that clarification.

CHRIS: I . . . I got accepted into the teaching program at Albright.

JASON: What? Come again?

CHRIS: Yeah. Starting in September. Yup! Plan on working double shifts. Put away a little something, you know, for tuition.

STAN: Good for you!

JASON: Wait . . . Wait, no way. Dude, what the fuck are you saying? Why didn't you tell me?

CHRIS: Cuz, I knew you'd make fun of me.

JASON: Of course I will. Whatcha gonna do? Teach history at Reading High for the next twenty years?

CHRIS: I might.

JASON: Yeah? You'll fucking suck.

CHRIS: You know what? You need to shut up an' drink your beer. That's exactly why I didn't say anything.

JASON: Whatever. In four years, max, guarantee you'll be back begging for your job at Olstead's. And yo, have you been up to Reading High lately? It's like a prison yard, they got thirty-year-old freshmen. Dude, that don't pay jack-shit, you'll have to take a second job just to keep your lights on.

STAN: He's got a point. Do you know what teachers make these days?

JASON: Tell him.

STAN: Seriously, son, not many people walk away from Olstead's, cuz you're not gonna find better money out there. You leave, it'll be impossible to get back in. They'll be ten guys lining up for your fucking job.

JASON: Yup.

STAN: That's the way it is. And I know a couple of the old guys who are bringing in close to forty-something dollars an hour.

JASON: Listen.

STAN: Teaching, well—

CHRIS: That's cool. Good for them. But, I kinda wanna do something a little different than my moms and pops. Yo, I got aspirations. There it is. And I won't apologize.

JASON: You got aspirations? What is this, Black History Month?

CHRIS: As a matter of fact it is. You got a problem with that?

JASON: If we're being perfectly honest, I get a little tired of the syrupy commercials. Actually, it shouldn't be called Black History Month, it should be called "Make White People Feel Guilty Month." Right, Stan?

STAN: Don't pull me into this.

JASON: And how come there's no White History Month?

CHRIS: Psh. I'm gonna let you ponder that question! Which may be a little difficult for you, I know, and I'm sorry.

JASON: Fuck you. You haven't even gone to college and you're already an asshole.

CHRIS: No offense, but I'm fucking sick of jacking. Phomp. Phomp. Phomp. The machines are so fucking loud I can't even think. It's getting harder and harder to pull myself up and go to work every day.

JASON: You're tripping.

STAN: I hear you, but the trick is, you gotta find a rhythm and stay inside of it, that's how you manage.

CHRIS: Well, it ain't a rhythm I wanna learn.

JASON: What the floor, it ain't good enough for you?!

CHRIS: Don't get it twisted, I'm not saying that. But . . .

JASON: What?

CHRIS: You ain't noticed the shit that's been going on.

JASON: What are you talking about?

CHRIS: I dunno. Forget it. But—

JASON: Don't do that! C'mon. What?

CHRIS: Like, last week, remember, they had a couple of them white hats walking the floor.

JASON: Yeah, so? Dude, maybe they're just upgrading the equipment.

CHRIS: Well, they got buttons now, BOOP, that can replace all of us. Boop. Boop.

JASON: C'mon, you're being paranoid.

CHRIS: Man, you ever given any thought to what you might do if this don't work out?

JASON: . . . Nah, not really. Knock on wood. I plan on retiring from the plant when I'm like fifty with a killa pension and money to burn, buy a condo in Myrtle Beach, open a Dunkin' Donuts and live my life. Right, Stan?

STAN: Not a bad plan.

CHRIS: Really? Dunkin' Donuts, that's your vision, huh? Dunkin'-Fuckin'-Donuts?

JASON: Yeah, so?

CHRIS: Punch in, punch out, and at the end of the day you end up with a box of donuts and diabetes. My man, where's your imagination? You need to get on a bus and do some traveling.

JASON: What about our cruise to Jamaica? Quit whining.

(A moment.)

But seriously, man, why didn't you tell me?

CHRIS: Cuz—

JASON: Shit, I just kinda thought we'd retire and open a franchise together. We're a team, you can't leave!!

CHRIS: Yeah, I can.

JASON: What about me?

CHRIS: What about you?

JASON: You coulda told me.

CHRIS: Dude, it's just something I gotta do.

JASON: Yeah, right!

CHRIS: What?

JASON: Okay.

CHRIS: What?!

JASON: Whatever. Hey Stan, pour this bitch a shot so he'll shut the fuck up.

SCENE 4

March 2, 2000

Outside it's 48°F.

In the news: In the Republican Presidential Debate, Alan Keyes, John McCain and George Bush. In Reading, an overnight fire leaves a mother with five children homeless. Baldwin Hardware Corporation, a brass hardware maker, announces plans to open a new 280,000-square-foot facility in Leesport.

Lights up. Bar. Brucie (African-American, forties) sits at the bar nursing a drink. The Republican Debate (Keyes, McCain, Bush) plays on the television.

STAN: Who are you liking?

BRUCIE: Don't matter. They'll all shit on us in the end.

STAN: What do you think of this Bush guy?

BRUCIE: I dunno. He looks like a little fucking chimp. But, if
    I gotta go with someone, Bradley's my man. Always liked

him, cut through the bullshit, got to the ball, kept it up in the air.

STAN: Yeah, for sure, a real smart player. Like 'im, don't know how good a president he'd be, but I'd want him in a pickup game. You watching this?

BRUCIE: Nah.

(Stan channel-surfs, grows bored, then switches off the television. Oscar enters and begins replenishing the bar. He works silently and methodically, actively listening to the conversation. His quiet but alert presence should be felt throughout the scene.)

You see Garth?

STAN: Nah, what's up?

BRUCIE: He opened a B and B.

STAN: Get outta here, you're the third person to tell me that.

BRUCIE: He always said he was gonna do it. He used to talk about it all of the time. "A bed-and-breakfast in Honduras. It's gonna be dope, y'all." I was, like, "What? Yeah, where the fuck is Honduras?" Garth was a cheap-ass bastard. He would never buy a round. Now, I get it.

STAN: Eyes on the prize.

BRUCIE: Yeah.

STAN: Whatcha up to?

BRUCIE: Shit, you know—

STAN: Yeah—

BRUCIE: Out there. I don't wanna go backwards.

STAN: I hear that, so how many days you guys been locked out?

BRUCIE: Ninety-three weeks.

STAN: That's what I thought. Tough.

BRUCIE: Yup. Didn't wanna take the new contract. Be a fucking slave. That's what they want. We offered to take a fifty-percent pay cut, they won't budge, they want us to give up our retirement. What's the point? Full circle, a lifetime, and be the same place I was when I was eighteen. What is that?

STAN: They bring in temps?

BRUCIE: Yeah, mostly Spanish cats, whatever. Cross the line, they work 'em to the bone, then get a fresh batch in three months.

STAN: Fuck 'em, you can do better.

BRUCIE: I know a coupla cats have moved on, but if we win this new contract at the textile mill, there's a big payout. That's why I'm holding out. They're trying to break the union.

STAN: Can't be done. I'm proud of you guys.

BRUCIE: It's pointless.

STAN: Don't say that.

BRUCIE: I been on the hustle for how many years? Worked hard. Right? Had the family. Now, I'm forty-nine.

STAN: Get outta here.

BRUCIE: Yeah, forty-fucking-nine, but listen, I was thinking the other day, I gotta do this for the next, what? fifteen–twenty years. You know this! Worrying. The hustle, man, my pop didn't go through this shit. I mean, he . . . he clocked in every day until he didn't, and went out with a nice package. He went on an eighteen-day cruise through the Greek Islands last October. Me, shit, I run the full mile, I put in the time, do the right thing, don't get me wrong, I had some good years . . . But, dude, tell me what I did wrong, huh?

STAN: I hear you. Getting injured was the best thing that ever happened to me. Got me out of that vortex. Three generations on the floor. Loyal as hell, I never imagined working anywhere else. I get injured. I'm in the hospital for nearly two months. I can't walk. Can't feel my toes. Not one of those Olstead fuckers called to check on me, to say, "I'm sorry for not fixing the machine." They knew that machine was trouble. Ramsey, Smitz—everyone wrote it up.

BRUCIE: I know how that goes.

STAN: The only time I heard from Olstead is when they sent their hard-ass lawyer to the hospital, 'cause they didn't want me to sue. Fucking pricks. Twenty-eight years. That's when I understood. That's when I knew, I was nobody to them. Nobody! Three generations of loyalty to the same company. This is America, right? You'd think that would mean something. They behave like they're doing you a goddamn favor.

BRUCIE: I hear you.

STAN: Bottom line, they don't understand that human decency is at the core of everything. I been jacking all them years and I can count on my hand the number of times they said thank you. Management: look me in the eye, say "thank you" now and then. "Thanks, Stan, for coming in early and working on the weekend. Good job." I loved my job. I was good at my job. Twenty-eight years jacking. And look at my leg! That's what I get.

BRUCIE: I feel you. But can I be real honest? . . .

STAN: Yeah, of course.

BRUCIE *(Raw and honest)*: . . . I don't know what to do.

STAN: Whatcha mean?

BRUCIE: I don't know what to do? *(Meaning: "What's my purpose?")* You know . . . I don't know anymore. What's the point? You know? I'm being dead serious.

STAN: You can't think that way.

BRUCIE: This is *me* being honest. I mean, what's the fucking point? Huh?

STAN: Things'll pick up.

BRUCIE *(With edge)*: Yeah, you think so?!

STAN: I do.

BRUCIE: I'm not receiving that message! Last week, I was at the union office signing up for some bullshit training and this old white cat, whatever, gets in my face, talking about how we took his job. We? I asked him who he was talking about, and he pointed at me. ME? So I said, if you ain't noticed I'm in the same fucking line as you. Hello?! You'd think that would shut him down. But, no. He's a scratch in the vinyl, going on and on about us coming here and ruining everything. Like I'm fresh off the boat or some shit. He don't know my biography. October 2nd, 1952, my father picked his last bale of cotton. He packed his razor and a Bible and headed North. Ten days later he had a job at Dixon's Hosieries. He clawed his way up from the filth of the yard to Union Rep, fighting for fucking assholes just like that cat. So, I don't understand it. This damn blame game, I got enough of that in my marriage.

STAN: Don't worry about it.

(Cynthia, Tracey and Jessie enter, in the midst of conversation.)

TRACEY: Fill her up, Stan!

BRUCIE: Cynth.

CYNTHIA: What are you doing here?!

BRUCIE: Same as you, getting a drink.

CYNTHIA: Here?

BRUCIE: Hey Jessie, Tracey.

JESSIE: Brucie.

TRACEY: What's up?

BRUCIE: Not much. You guys look good.

TRACEY: You've always been a sweet liar.

BRUCIE: Hey Cynth, you got a minute?

CYNTHIA: No.

BRUCIE: Just—

CYNTHIA: No!

(Cynthia plops down with Jessie and Tracey.)

It's been a long day. I don't wanna start. Let me have a drink. K?

TRACEY: Ignore 'im.

JESSIE: Don't worry about it, we'll get one drink and then go. K?

(Brucie approaches the women.)

BRUCIE: C'mon, Cynth—

CYNTHIA: What do you want?

BRUCIE: Can I talk to you?

CYNTHIA: No.

BRUCIE: Can I talk to you?!

CYNTHIA: No!

BRUCIE: CAN I TALK TO YOU?

CYNTHIA: NO!

(Brucie slams the table. It's jarring. The women stand in unison, a united front.)

STAN: C'mon, Brucie. Sit down. You want another drink?

TRACEY: She doesn't want to talk to you.

BRUCIE: You stay outta this!

STAN: Hey. Hey. C'mon—

TRACEY: Let's go.

CYNTHIA: I'm not going. This is my place.

JESSIE: That's right.

BRUCIE: Let's just talk.

CYNTHIA: I know what you want. Don't have it.

(Cynthia turns her pockets inside out.)

BRUCIE: Nice show. I heard you're—

CYNTHIA: What?

BRUCIE: We gotta do this in front of everyone?

CYNTHIA: We don't gotta do this at all. I don't recall having anything to say to you.

TRACEY: Relax, ignore him.   JESSIE: Don't listen, don't!

STAN: Come on, let me buy you one . . . It's okay. What're you drinking?

(De-escalating.)

BRUCIE: Same.

STAN: C'mon, sit. Let it go. Don't worry.

(Tense. Stan pours Brucie a drink.)

BRUCIE *(To Stan)*: She's playing games.
STAN: Don't worry about it.
CYNTHIA: He's like clockwork. Thursday. Paycheck.
TRACEY: You want me to talk to him?
CYNTHIA: Nah. It'll just make him crazier.

(Brucie stares at Cynthia.)

TRACEY: Don't even look at him.
CYNTHIA: He's gonna sit there just to fuck with me.
JESSIE: Stay strong!

(The women actively ignore Brucie as he tries to get Cynthia's attention. He mouths, "Cynthia." Finally:)

(To Brucie) Why don't you leave her alone?!
BRUCIE: Why don't you relax your mouth?!
CYNTHIA: Don't talk to her that way!

(Brucie demonstratively places his hands over his heart.)

BRUCIE: Cynth? Babe?
STAN: Brucie . . .
BRUCIE: You're not being fair.
CYNTHIA: Who's not being fair?! Where are my muthafucking fish, Brucie? Huh?

(Cynthia suddenly gets up from the table and marches toward Brucie.)

TRACEY: Don't.   JESSIE *(To Brucie)*: You got
                                         some nerve!

BRUCIE: Just wanna talk.
CYNTHIA: Here I am! Talk!

(Brucie gently takes her hand.)

TRACEY: Cynthia!
BRUCIE: Hey, mouth, give us a second.
TRACEY: You don't have any respect for women.
BRUCIE: No, I don't have no respect for you. So shut up!
TRACEY: And *you* wonder why your wife won't talk to you.
BRUCIE: . . . Can you just give us some room?
CYNTHIA *(To Tracy)*: I got this.

(A moment.)

What do you want, Brucie?
BRUCIE: I keep trying to explain.

(Brucie produces a piece of paper.)

CYNTHIA: What's that?

(He hands it to Cynthia. She reads.)

BRUCIE: I'm in a program.
CYNTHIA: And is having a drink part of that program?
BRUCIE: It's not the same.
CYNTHIA: I beg to differ.
BRUCIE: That's all you gotta say?
CYNTHIA: Whatcha want me to say?
BRUCIE: Just wanna show you I'm trying.
CYNTHIA: K.
BRUCIE: And?
CYNTHIA: We done?

(Brucie folds the paper and puts it in his pocket.)

BRUCIE: Yeah.

CYNTHIA: K. Nice piece of paper. Maybe I'd be impressed if it was a pay stub. You call your son?

BRUCIE: How's he doing?

CYNTHIA: Good. Evolution. Chris tell you his news?

BRUCIE: Nah.

CYNTHIA: He got into Albright.

BRUCIE: Psh, for real?

CYNTHIA: That's all you gotta say? You know, he really wants you to . . . Forget it, just call 'im. K. He's starting in September.

BRUCIE: College? Who's paying for it?

CYNTHIA: He is.

BRUCIE: You gonna let him walk away from that steady money at the plant? Ask me, he'd be a damn fool to—

CYNTHIA: Good advice. How's that working out for you?

BRUCIE: . . .

CYNTHIA: Look, if you speak to him, do me a favor, say you're proud of 'im and leave it at that. Don't put any other ideas in his head. Cuz if you do, so help me God . . . This is a good thing. And you should be proud of him.

TRACEY: That's right, he's always been smart, Cynth.

BRUCIE: I'm just saying—

CYNTHIA: Say nothing for a change.

(A moment.)

BRUCIE: You doing okay?

CYNTHIA: Yeah. I'm cool.

BRUCIE: Stan says you're being considered for a promotion.

CYNTHIA: Yeah. Warehouse Supervisor. Not just me. Tracey, Clarence and Fat Henry. We're all in the running.

BRUCIE *(To Tracey)*: That true?

TRACEY: Yeah. Deciding soon. But, I'm not holding my breath, they're just blowing smoke up our asses, because some fancy consultant told 'em it would be a good idea to chum the waters.

CYNTHIA: C'mon. You want this as bad as I do. You won't own it, but I know you do.

JESSIE: Of course she does, Tracey likes giving fucking orders.

TRACEY: Get outta here.   CYNTHIA: But, c'mon if one us
                                 gets this job, how sweet'll
                                 that be?

(Cynthia gives Tracey a warm hug.)

BRUCIE *(Humor with edge)*: They must be hard up if they're considering you guys.

CYNTHIA: Don't start with me. Listen, I'm glad you're getting things together. But, I got—

BRUCIE: Wait a minute, wait a minute. Don't walk away. Please. I feel bad about what went down in December. It wasn't me . . . I'm sorry. Look, I'm getting clean. Okay? It's not gonna happen again. It's too embarrassing. You know me. Psh. I useta make fun of cats like me.

(He takes her hand. Smooth. Cynthia is vulnerable to his charm.)

I'm sorry. K, babe? You look good. You always looked sexy in your work clothing.

JESSIE: Tracey, do something.

BRUCIE: I couldn't help but notice when I was by the house that the gutter needs to be rehung. I can come by and do it. We'll keep things simple, you know, talk. I feel like if things was good with us, it would be easier to get back on my feet.

CYNTHIA: Don't think so. You can call Chris . . . Get off that dope, but don't come by.

BRUCIE: When I get my job back—

CYNTHIA: If. If. I'm all for you guys standing strong, babe, but at some point you gotta think about what this is doing to us.

BRUCIE *(All smoothness)*: Can I get a kiss?

CYNTHIA: What?

BRUCIE: Can I at least get a kiss?

(He goes in for a kiss, Cynthia surrenders. An intimate moment. Then Tracey jumps to attention.)

TRACEY: I think you better go!

BRUCIE: I'm not talking to you, mouth!

TRACEY: You're talking to her, you're talking to me.

BRUCIE: You got a lotta moxie for a white girl.

TRACEY: I got more than moxie! Try me! Leave her alone. Okay? She's doing really well—

JESSIE: Don't fuck this up for her!

TRACEY: You wanna do something for Cynthia? Get clean or get lost. That's the best thing you can do for her.

BRUCIE: Don't you tell me what I need to do! I know what I need to do!

STAN: Brucie, maybe you better—

(Brucie is suddenly emotional. He tries to pull it together, but he's battling a tsunami.)

BRUCIE: Cynthia! Please—

CYNTHIA: No!!

SCENE 5

April 17, 2000

Outside it's 60°F.
   In the news: Three days after a record 617-point drop in the Dow Jones as the tech bubble bursts. DC protesters disrupt the World Bank and International Monetary Fund meeting. A 26-year-old man is shot leaving a bar on Woodward Street in Reading.
   Bar exterior. Tracey stands outside, smoking a cigarette. Oscar steps outside and stands in the doorway.

OSCAR: Hey.
TRACEY: Hey.
OSCAR: Can I bum a cigarette?
TRACEY *(Dismissive)*: No.
OSCAR: Thank you for nothing.
TRACEY: You're welcome.

(Beat. Oscar is still standing in the doorway.)

Don't you got something to do?
OSCAR: It's my break.

(An awkward moment.)

Did you know they're waiting for you inside?
TRACEY: Yeah, I know.
OSCAR: Do you want me to tell 'em you're out here?
TRACEY: Do I look like I need you to mind my business?
OSCAR: Okay, whatever. Just trying to help.
TRACEY: Can you, like, give me my space?
OSCAR: Technically, this is my space. This is where I chill. This
is my spot. But, I'm a gentleman.
TRACEY: Good for you. Now, fuck off.
OSCAR *(Under his breath)*: Bitch.
TRACEY: Asshole.
OSCAR: Fuck you.
TRACEY: No, fuck you!

(A brief standoff, neither will surrender ground.)

. . . What?
OSCAR: What?!

(Finally, Tracey melts and gives him a cigarette.)

TRACEY: Happy?
OSCAR: Thank you.

(She lights his cigarette. They smoke.)

. . . You—
TRACEY: Yeah?
OSCAR: Um. Um, uh, uh—

TRACEY: Are you retarded? What?

OSCAR: You work at the plant, right?

TRACEY: Along with everyone else who comes in here. Dah!

OSCAR: It awright?

TRACEY: It's okay, it's a job. Steady. Whatever.

OSCAR: They pay good?

TRACEY: I pay my bills. What's with all the questions?

OSCAR: I'm just asking cuz I saw a posting down at the Centro Hispano.

TRACEY: What the fuck is that?

OSCAR: The Latino Community Center.

TRACEY: What do you mean you saw a posting?

OSCAR: A posting, a job posting. Olstead's? Steel Tubing? That's your place, right?

TRACEY: It's not my place, it's where I work.

OSCAR: Yeah, okay . . . they're looking to hire folks, and I know it gotta pay better than here.

TRACEY: What are you talking about? Olstead's isn't hiring.

OSCAR: That ain't what I heard. They's looking to train packers, shippers . . . I got the info.

(Oscar takes a folded flyer from his pocket.)

TRACEY: Let me see that.

(Tracey takes the flyer.)

All I can read is "Olstead's." The rest is gibberish.

OSCAR: No it's Spanish. See there, it gives times when you go down to the plant to fill out an application for training.

TRACEY: This is a joke. I don't think so. No. No. First off, you gotta be in the union.

OSCAR: Not according to the flyer.

TRACEY: Well, you got it wrong.

OSCAR: Okay.

TRACEY: You got it wrong!

OSCAR: Okay!

TRACEY: *And* that's not how it works. Anyway. You gotta know somebody to get in. My dad worked there, I work there and my son works there. It's that kinda shop. Always been.

OSCAR: I know you.

TRACEY: You don't know me.

OSCAR: How does someone get in?

TRACEY: Enough with the questions. Your mother didn't teach you to respect your elders?

OSCAR: They're getting pretty lit in there.

TRACEY: Yeah?

OSCAR: Sooo, what are they celebrating?

TRACEY: You know Cynthia.

OSCAR: Yeah.

TRACEY: Well, she just got promoted last week. They gave her a frigging cushion of a job. A recliner. And I wish she'd just shut up about it already.

OSCAR: I thought you guys was friends.

TRACEY: Yeah, we're friends. So? You don't get sick of your friends sometimes?

(Tracey draws on her cigarette.)

You know how long I been working at the plant? Forget it . . . Never mind, it's not important . . . But, I know the floor as good as Cynthia. I do. You wanna know the truth, the only reason I didn't get the job is because Butz tried to fuck me and I wouldn't let him, and he told everyone in management that I'm unstable. I'm not unstable. I'm like—

OSCAR: That's some shit.

TRACEY: Yeah. It sucks. And, I betcha they wanted a minority. I'm not prejudice, but that's how things are going these days. I got eyes. They get tax breaks or something.

OSCAR: I dunno know about all that.

TRACEY: It's a fact. That's how things are going. And I'm not prejudice, I say, you are who you are, you know? I'm cool with everyone. But, I mean . . . c'mon . . . you guys coming over here, you can get a job faster than—

OSCAR: I was born here.

TRACEY: Still . . . you wasn't born here, Berks.

OSCAR: Yeah, I was.

TRACEY: Yeah? Well, my family's been here a long time. Since the twenties, okay? They built the house that I live in. They built this town. My grandfather was German, and he could build anything. Cabinets, fine furniture, anything. He had these amazing hands. Sturdy. Meaty. Real firm. You couldn't shake his hand without feeling his presence, feeling his power. And those hands, let me tell you, they were solid, worker hands, you know, and they really, really knew how to make things. Beautiful things. I'm not talking about now, how you got these guys who can patch a hole with spackle and think they're the shit. My grandfather was the real thing. A craftsman . . . And I remember when I was a kid, I mean eight or nine, we'd go downtown to Penn with Opa. To walk and look in store windows. Downtown was real nice back then. You'd get dressed up to go shopping. You know, Pomeroy's, Whitner's, whatever. I felt really special, because he was this big, strapping man and people gave him room. But, what I really loved was that he'd take me to office buildings, banks . . . you name it, and he'd point out the woodwork. And if you got really, really close he'd show some detail that he'd carved for me. An apple blossom. Really. That's what I'm talking about. It was back when if you worked with your hands people respected you for it. It was a gift. But now, there's nothing on Penn. You go into the buildings, the walls are covered over with sheetrock, the wood painted gray, or some ungodly color, and it just makes me sad. It makes me . . . Whatever.

OSCAR: You okay?

TRACEY: Listen, that piece of paper that you're holding is an insult, it don't mean anything, Olstead's isn't for you.

SCENE 6

May 5, 2000

Outside it's 84°F.
> *In the news: The U.S. unemployment rate tumbles to a 30-year low, 3.9%. The City of Reading fires a dozen employees, fearing a deficit of $10,000,000. Allen Iverson and the Philadelphia 76ers prepare for Game 1 of the Eastern Conference Semifinals.*
> *Lights up. Bar. Stan prepares a gimlet. Jessie sits at the bar eyeing a birthday cake. Oscar is behind the bar, playing a portable video game.*

STAN: A gimlet, shaken but not stirred.

> *(Stan places the cocktail on the bar.)*

JESSIE: Did you actually put some alcohol in it this time?
STAN: Against my better judgment, I did—

JESSIE: Very funny.

(*Jessie takes a sip, savoring.*)

STAN: You been warming that seat for a long time. Are the ladies
coming?

JESSIE: That's what they say, but who knows at this point?

STAN: What time were they supposed to meet ya?

JESSIE: Officially? Over an hour ago.

STAN: Jesus. Is something going on that I should know?

JESSIE: Dunno. Cynthia. The promotion. Whatever. Tracey
pretends like it ain't a big deal. But, I can tell she don't
like taking orders from Cynthia. And don't spread this, but
things haven't been so good between them.

STAN: That's the way people are in this town. Bitch and moan,
want something better. But, then the minute someone does
well, forget it.

JESSIE: Tell me about it. Tracey's been going around town
whispering that the only reason Cynthia got the job is cuz
she's black. Two months ago she couldn't give a shit, and
suddenly—

STAN: C'mon. Bullshit. Cynthia earned that promotion.

JESSIE: Sure, but I know for a fact that it pissed off a lot of people.

STAN: Gimme a break. People don't like change. I wouldn't lose
any sleep over it—

JESSIE: You're right, fuck 'em all, I'm sick of being in the middle. Let's cut the cake.

STAN: You sure?

JESSIE: Yeah!

STAN: Hey, Oscar.

OSCAR: Yeah?

STAN: Will you get me a knife?

(*Oscar retrieves a knife from the bar.*)

You got any special birthday wishes?

JESSIE: Hell yeah. But, you know what would be nice, a kiss. I just wanna be kissed today.

(Jessie blows out the candles.)

STAN: Happy birthday, sweetheart.
OSCAR: Happy birthday.
JESSIE: Thank you.

(Jessie cuts the cake. Cynthia rushes in, winded.)

CYNTHIA: I'm so sorry, babe.
JESSIE: Here comes the boss!
CYNTHIA: What a headache, I got stuck at a meeting.
JESSIE: Everything okay?
CYNTHIA: Don't worry about it. Today is your day. Here. Happy birthday.

(Cynthia passes Jessie a Cher CD.)

(Singing:)
Do you believe in life after love?

(Cynthia hugs Jessie. They both sing:)

CYNTHIA AND JESSIE:
I can feel something inside me say
I really don't think you're strong enough.

JESSIE: I almost forgive you.
CYNTHIA: There's no way I'd miss this, but I couldn't get out of there. I was trapped in a room of "supervisors," all of 'em had passionate ideas about how the floor could be run more efficiently, yet none of those donkeys have actually operated a machine.
JESSIE: No shit.

CYNTHIA: There's this one idiot who seriously thinks that the plant can be run by five and a half people.

JESSIE: Ha! Where are you going to find half a person?

STAN: Whiskey?

CYNTHIA: Double, babe.

STAN *(Sarcastically)*: Jeez, how's the new job?

CYNTHIA: Exhausting.

JESSIE: As long as they fix the air-conditioning this summer, I'm happy.

CYNTHIA: It's number sixteen on my very long list, babe, don't hold your breath.

STAN: Look at you. You got a list?

CYNTHIA: I also got a desk, whoa, and a computer.

STAN: What?!

JESSIE: I seen it, she ain't lying.

STAN: I mean shit, all of them years on the floor. That must taste sweet.

CYNTHIA: Sweet don't even begin to describe it, babe. First day, I park. Get out, and immediately head for the floor, it's a reflex. I just do it, get to the door, same as usual, I smell the oil and metal dust, I hear the machinery churning and feel the energy of the room. I go to my station, say, "Hey Lance, Becky," get ready, my body knows it's there to pack tubes. That's what I do.

STAN: // That's what you do.

CYNTHIA: I fire up the machine, but everyone is looking at me, and Tracey says, "What the fuck you doing here?" Then I remember. I can go sit down.

JESSIE: // Yes, you can

CYNTHIA: I'm not wearing my Carhartt, not gonna be on my feet for ten hours, I loosen my support belt, I don't have to worry about my fingers cramping or the blood blister on my left foot. I can stop sweating because goddamn the office has air-conditioning. These muthafuckers got air-conditioning.

JESSIE: Of course they do.

CYNTHIA: Twenty-four years, and I can't remember talking to anyone in the office, except to do paperwork. I mean some of these folks have been working there as long as us, but they're as unfamiliar as a stranger sitting next to you on a bus.

JESSIE: That's for sure.

STAN: Yeah—

CYNTHIA: It's like looking at a map, and discovering that you're only just a few miles away from the ocean. But you didn't know because it was on the other side of the damn mountains.

JESSIE: I'm so proud of you. You got off the fucking floor.

(Chris and Jason sweep in with energy and hug Jessie. Suddenly it's a party.)

CHRIS: WHASSUP?!

JASON: We miss the party?!

JESSIE: Nah. You're just in time, we're cutting the cake.

JASON: Looks good.

(Jason swipes frosting with his fingers.)

STAN: Hey, get outta there.

JASON: Happy birthday!	CHRIS *(Singing)*: "Happy birthday to ya!"
JESSIE: Thank you!	CYNTHIA: Where you guys coming from?

CHRIS: Just took a spin on Jason's new bike.

STAN: No!

JASON: Yes!

STAN: Congratulations!	CYNTHIA: I hope you were wearing a helmet.

CHRIS *(To Stan)*: Whatcha got on tap?

STAN: You need to ask?

CHRIS: Keep hope alive. That's all I'm saying.

JASON: Dude.

(Jason scans the room.)

Where's Ma?

JESSIE: I dunno, you tell me.

JASON: Don't worry. She'll be here. You know her.

JESSIE: Yeah.   CHRIS *(To Cynthia)*: You look
all important.

CYNTHIA: Gotta dress the part.

(Chris gives Cynthia a hug.)

JESSIE: Betcha proud of your ma?

CHRIS: She's aight.

(Cynthia gives Chris a playful jab.)

JESSIE *(To Cynthia)*: Hey Cynth, you remember the first day we met? You were sporting an afro and platforms and I thought there's no way you were gonna make a day on the line.

CYNTHIA: And you looked like fucking Joni Mitchell with a headband and hair down to your butt.

JESSIE: Guess how old I was when I started, Stan?

STAN: Nineteen—

JESSIE: Eighteen. Eighteen! Can you believe it? The summer I started, I was a couple years younger than you guys!

JASON: Betcha were hot.

JESSIE: You know, I was.

STAN: She was.

JESSIE: God, that was a summer, huh? A lot of fun. Wasn't thinking about anything, I figured I'd be at Olstead's for six to eight months max. Can you believe it? I was collecting Green Stamps the whole year, remember Green Stamps? I was gonna trade 'em in for a backpack, a tent. Had like ten thousand of 'em. I was going to hitch my way across the country with my boyfriend, Felix.

CYNTHIA: Felix. I remember Felix, he was a musician, right?

JESSIE: He had a harmonica. And we planned to wind up in Alaska where my dad worked in a cannery. Kodiak.

STAN: I knew your dad, Phil Lombardi, he looked liked, um—

JESSIE: James Garner.

STAN: Yeah. That's right.

JESSIE: He split for Alaska when I was thirteen. A lotta folks went up there that summer. Remember?

STAN: Sure.

JESSIE: God. Me. Felix. That was so long ago. We were gonna do Alaska, camp, live clean, you know, and save enough money to get to India. Live in an ashram for a while, then bum along the hippie trail. Istanbul, Tehran, Kandahar, Kabul, Peshawar, Lahore, Kathmandu. Places. Still remember 'em all. I used to say 'em every night like a mantra, a prayer: Istanbul, Tehran, Kandahar, Kabul, Peshawar, Lahore, Kathmandu. I mapped the whole thing out. Yeah, we had this, um, world map, that Felix had ripped outta an atlas in the library. *The World Book*. God . . . That was the plan.

JASON: So, why didn't you go?

JESSIE: Started working, met Dan, I guess I got caught in the riptide, couldn't get back to shore. That's how it is.

CHRIS: You ever sorry?

(The weight of the question lands on Jessie.)

JESSIE: I guess, I wish . . . I had gotten to see the world. You know, left Berks, if only for a year. That's what I regret. Not the work, I regret the fact that for a little while it seemed like, I don't know, there was possibility. I think about that Jessie on the other side of the world and what she woulda seen.

(Surprising emotions.)

Whoa. I'm sorry. I didn't see that coming.
STAN: Look, I got to see a little of the world after 'Nam. Shit follows you everywhere. In some ways you're better off not knowing.
JESSIE: Yeah? You don't know what you don't know, until you wanna know, right? And then it's too late. Istanbul, Tehran, Kandahar, Kabul, Peshawar, Lahore, Kathmandu.

(Tracey enters with a flurry of energy.)

STAN: There she is!
TRACEY: The party can officially begin!
CYNTHIA: Look who finally showed up.

(Tracey and Jessie hug.)

JESSIE *(Smiling)*: Thank you for making room for us.
CYNTHIA *(Offhanded)*: Yeah! You get lost on your way over?
TRACEY: Gimme a break, I'm here. Okay. I'm sorry. Get over it!

(Tracey gives Cynthia a cutting glance.)

JESSIE: C'mon, you guys. We're here to celebrate! Both of you get over it. Okay? Calm down. It's my birthday. I'm just happy my besties are here.
CYNTHIA: She brought the attitude. I was chill—
TRACEY: What's your problem? Relax. Jason, get your ma a beer.
JASON: Ma?!!
TRACEY: C'mon, c'mon.

(She hugs him.)

I love you!!!

(Jason walks over to the bar.)

JASON: A pint.

(Stan pours a beer.)

JESSIE: You okay?

TRACEY: Why wouldn't I be okay?

JESSIE: I don't know, you just—

TRACEY: What? I'm fine. Let's celebrate. Yahoo!

JESSIE: Suddenly, it doesn't feel like a celebration.

(Chris searches for a song on the jukebox. Jason digs into a slice of cake.)

TRACEY: Why are you making such a big deal? I'm late. I'm sorry. I'm here.

(A moment. Jason gives Tracey the beer. Tracey visibly avoids sitting next to Cynthia.)

CYNTHIA: Hey, Tracey. We good? Cuz since all of this went down I definitely feel some tension. Maybe I'm making it up, but . . . We've been friends a long time, you've always been straight with me. You got a problem, tell me.

TRACEY: Yeah?

CYNTHIA: I'm sorry, but I don't know why I'm catching shade? What's up?

TRACEY: Now's not the time for this. K.

CYNTHIA: I took this promotion cuz I thought it would be good for all of us.

TRACEY: Yeah, right?!

CYNTHIA: And I don't deserve the things you've been saying. You've always been cool. Be angry, but don't make it about this . . . *(Points to the skin on the back of her hand)* Look at me, Tracey. You don't want to go down that road, we've got too much history between us. You got a problem, you tell me to my face.

TRACEY: I just feel like, um . . . I . . . I see you getting pretty chummy with "them" . . . And . . . The other day on the floor I called out to you, but you brushed me off.

CYNTHIA: I gotta look busy, that's half the job, babe.

TRACEY: I know that, but it's the way you did it.

CYNTHIA: Well, I'm sorry! I'm learning. Cut me some slack, okay? There's a lotta pressure on me right now. // They're watching.

TRACEY: Yeah?

CYNTHIA: Yeah!

JESSIE: C'mon guys, let's not do this.

TRACEY: . . . And is there something you aren't telling us?

CYNTHIA: What do you mean?

TRACEY: I dunno.

CYNTHIA: C'mon, don't play games.

TRACEY: Are they gonna be laying people off?

JASON: Whoa!   CHRIS: Come again?

TRACEY: Answer me.

CYNTHIA: Where'd you hear that bullshit?

TRACEY: A little bird.

(They all look at Cynthia.)

CYNTHIA: . . .

TRACEY: Are they?

CYNTHIA: Look, there's been a little talk about trimming overhead, but there always is—

STAN: // Talk? We'll see about that.

CYNTHIA: I know what's important, don't think because I went upstairs that I can't see the grit on the floor. I got the same aches and pains as you guys. I wouldn't—

TRACEY: You'd tell us, right?

CYNTHIA: Of course.

TRACEY: Promise?!

CYNTHIA: Yes.

(Tracey pulls a flyer out of her pocket.)

TRACEY: Have you guys seen this flyer?

JESSIE: No.

CYNTHIA: No.   JASON: What is it?

TRACEY: When I first saw it I didn't believe it. Then a week ago, I saw a couple of these taped up at the gas station. Do you know what it says?

(Tracey shows Cynthia the flyer.)

CYNTHIA: It's in Spanish. I can't read it.

TRACEY: Hey Oscar.

OSCAR: Yeah?

(Tracey holds up the flyer.)

TRACEY: Do you wanna read this for Cynthia?

SCENE 7

July 4, 2000

Outside it's 84°F.

    In the news: Working Woman *magazine reports that the salary gap is narrowing between men and women in some U.S. industries. Reading police crack down on high-crime neighborhoods in response to a recent rise in violent crime. The City of Reading purchases a number of run-down buildings with plans to demolish them in an effort to combat urban blight.*

    Outside the bar. Brucie smokes a cigarette, clearly high. Chris and Jason rush out of the bar, past him. Bottle rockets explode in the distance.

BRUCIE: Chris! Chris! Your mom inside?

CHRIS: No, but give her some space, she don't want to talk to you . . .

BRUCIE: Hold up. You got a minute?

CHRIS: No, gotta run.

BRUCIE: What's the rush?

CHRIS: Something's going on down at the plant.

JASON: C'mon, Chris. // Let's move.

BRUCIE: It'll only take a minute.

JASON: Yo!

CHRIS: Quick—

BRUCIE: I was just wondering whether you could spot me—

CHRIS: Now's not a good time.

JASON: Yo! Let's—

BRUCIE (*Smiling*): Gotcha, but it only takes five seconds to reach into your pocket.

CHRIS: Yeah, and a whole week of work to replace what's in there.

BRUCIE: What about you, Jason?

JASON: Sorry, Brucie.

BRUCIE: I'm getting some benefits next week. The check hasn't come.

JASON: Can't do it.

BRUCIE: All right I hear you. But . . . Wait, wait, wait. Chris? C'mon?

(Chris gives Brucie a hug.)

CHRIS: Ten. That's all I can spare.

BRUCIE: Easy breezy, not complaining, thank you.

CHRIS: Listen, we really gotta go.

BRUCIE: Why are you rushing? What's happening?

JASON: Dunno, but Wilson says they moved three of the mills outta the factory over the long weekend.

BRUCIE: What?

JASON: Don't ask me. All I know is he passed by there about an hour ago to pick up something from his locker, and the machines were gone.

CHRIS: Gone . . .

JASON: Fucking assholes. He's calling everyone.

BRUCIE: What are you talking about?

CHRIS: Gone. Removed. // Gone.

JASON: Like not fucking there.

CHRIS: They posted a sign on the door, nobody was supposed to see it until tomorrow morning.

JASON: A list of names. Me, Chris—our names are on it.

BRUCIE: What do you think it means?

JASON: I don't know, but I'm gonna find out—

BRUCIE: Sly muthafuckas—

CHRIS: Makes you wanna hit somebody.

JASON: We're going by the plant, I wanna see it for myself.

BRUCIE: And your mom? She know about this?

CHRIS: Man, I hope she didn't.

(Brucie laughs, knowingly.)

What's funny?

BRUCIE: I'm not laughing at you, shit I'm just sorry to hear it. I know I'm not in the best position to give advice, but this is just the first step. They're gonna come at you. My two cents, take the small concessions.

CHRIS: What are you talkin' about?

BRUCIE: Cuz when we walked out of the textile mill thinking big, they locked us out, beat down our optimism and we couldn't get back in. And nearly two years later there ain't a damn thing we can do about it. Don't let them bring those temps in—fight it. Because once they do, you're out. You hear me? I wouldn't have said that six months ago, but I'm telling you truth.

JASON: Man, I pray it don't come to that.

BRUCIE: Get down on your knees, son . . .

JASON: . . . C'mon, Chris, let's move.

(Brucie holds out the ten dollars.)

BRUCIE: Here, I'll make do. Believe me, you're gonna need this. No machines, no jobs. That's pretty simple arithmetic.

JASON: Fuck // that!

CHRIS: Let's move.

ACT TWO

SCENE 1

October 13, 2008

Outside it's 79°F.

In the news: The Dow Jones gains 936 points, its largest gain ever, following news that the government-funded bank bailouts were approved around the world. In Berks County, Pennsylvania, power shutoffs for delinquent utility customers rise 111% over the previous year.

TRACEY: You gonna talk or are you waiting for me to dance for you?

JASON: It took a lot of nerve for me to ring the bell.

TRACEY: Ding dong, that's real hard.

JASON: I didn't wanna come, but I thought you might be kinda happy to see me. You got anything to drink?

TRACEY: Who told you, you could sit down?

JASON: I'm sitting cuz I'm tired.

TRACEY: Why the fuck did you do that to your face?

JASON: They're just tats. Get over it.

TRACEY: Well, it looks stupid.

(Tracey hands Jason five dollars.)

JASON: This is all you got?

TRACEY: You know what, leave it there. I don't need this shit right now. You call me up outta the blue: "Ma, I need money!" I almost didn't answer. What if I didn't answer? Huh? What would you do then?

(Jason examines the bill.)

JASON: Seriously? Five dollars, what's that, three cigarettes and a Slurpee? When I called you, you said you had money. I traveled all the way here for this? Fucking hell.

TRACEY: Sorry to inconvenience you. I had the money, but—

JASON: Shit. Really?

(A moment. It becomes evident that Tracey is strung out.)

How long has that been going on?

TRACEY: How long what?

JASON: Don't fuck with me, you know exactly what I'm talkin' about.

TRACEY: That's very rich coming from you. Gimme back my money, and get the fuck outta here.

JASON: You look like shit.

TRACEY: I look like shit? Have you looked in the mirror lately?

JASON: Is this really all you got?

TRACEY: Yeah. I'm not running a money farm.

JASON: I didn't believe Fat Henry when he said you were strung out.

TRACEY: Fat Henry needs to mind his business. It's for my back pain.

JASON: Aspirin won't do?

TRACEY: Ha, ha. Very funny. You have no idea. You . . . Have . . . No . . . Idea!

JASON: OKAY!

TRACEY: We done?

JASON: . . .

TRACEY: When can I git it back?

JASON: You want this five dollars back?

TRACEY: Yeah. I want it back. Tomorrow?

JASON: You know what, never mind. This is too much trouble.

TRACEY: Fine. Give it here.

(She grows antsy. She needs a fix. Jason extends the money, and she snatches it from him, desperate.)

JASON: Jesus, look at you.

TRACEY: What?!

JASON: How the fuck did this happen?

(Cynthia's sparse apartment. Cynthia, nervous and excited, scrambles into the room. She wears a nursing-home mainte-nance uniform. She picks up a couple of take-out food containers littering the floor.)

CHRIS: So. This is where you live?

CYNTHIA: Yeah. It's what I could manage for now. You hungry?

CHRIS: Nah. Where should I put my stuff?

CYNTHIA: Anywhere.

(Chris looks around. He drops his backpack.)

CHRIS: You didn't mention you moved.

CYNTHIA: No?

CHRIS: What happened to the house?

CYNTHIA: I got behind . . . You wanna drink or something?

CHRIS: Nah.

CYNTHIA: Why didn't you let me know you got out? I had to hear it from the grapevine.

CHRIS: I just needed some time. Still trying to get adjusted. Get my head back.

CYNTHIA: How long have you been out?

CHRIS: Six weeks?

CYNTHIA: Why didn't you call me? I woulda picked you up.

CHRIS: I dunno, I didn't wanna bother you.

CYNTHIA: Don't get it mixed up. You're staying here.

(Chris fidgets with the Bible in his hand.)

What's that?

CHRIS: It's my Bible.

CYNTHIA: A Bible?

CHRIS: Yeah, a Bible.

CYNTHIA: I heard you got all churchy.

CHRIS: I don't know what you heard, but this book saved my life.

CYNTHIA: Why don't you sit down? You're making me nervous just hovering there. Sit. Relax. You're home.

(Chris sits on the couch. Cynthia smiles, trying to break the ice.)

You got sorta mannish, huh? Put on weight since my last visit. You look different.

CHRIS: So do you. You okay?

CYNTHIA: Yeah. Yeah.

CHRIS: How are things?

CYNTHIA: Good. Good.

CHRIS: You, um, working?

CYNTHIA: I got some hours over at the university, maintenance. Also working at the nursing home, on weekends. Piecing things together. You know me, I'm a worker. Get restless otherwise.

CHRIS: Yeah. I walked around . . . Saw that Snookie's place closed.

CYNTHIA: Yeah.

CHRIS: Ran into . . . um . . .

CYNTHIA: Who?

CHRIS: Folks.

CYNTHIA: I'm sorry I couldn't get out to see you the last couple months, it got too expensive.

CHRIS: Um.

CYNTHIA: Everybody's been asking me about when you was getting out. But all those damn years you'd just become X's marked off on the calendar and it made me crazy. God . . . You know after everything. I wanna say that . . .

(Cynthia fights back emotions.)

I'm sorry.

CHRIS: For what?

CYNTHIA: It's just, I shoulda . . .

(Chris places his arms around Cynthia.)

CHRIS: C'mon. C'mon. I don't want this to be a big deal. Tell me about what's been going on. You hear from the old gang? Tracey?

CYNTHIA: Fuck her. After what went down. We don't really—

CHRIS: You hear, Jason's out.

CYNTHIA: Yeah? When did that happen?

CHRIS: Dunno. A couple months ago.

CYNTHIA: That little bastard. What did he have to say? He got you into this shit. If it wasn't for him . . . you'd . . . I coulda killed him.

CHRIS: It's done. I can't stay in that place.

CYNTHIA: Well, I'm still trying to understand what happened, Chris. What happened?

SCENE 2

July 17, 2000

Eight years earlier.
    Outside it's 82°F.
    In the news: Federal eligibility guidelines ease, allowing more families in Reading public schools to receive free and reduced school lunches. Several U.S. companies, including 3M, Johnson & Johnson, and General Electric, increase leadership development internally, expanding opportunities for minority employees.
    Bar. Loud arguing. Chris, Jason, Jessie, Tracey, Cynthia, Stan and Oscar in the bar.

CYNTHIA: Stop yelling! Stop yelling! // Stop yelling!
TRACEY: Tell us what's going on? // Tell us the truth!

    (Chris, Jason and Jessie raise their voices in agreement. Chaos. They continue to berate Cynthia.)

CYNTHIA: Stop shouting at me! Stop shouting. Listen. Listen. Listen! I'm tr . . . I'm trying.

TRACEY: What the hell is going on?!

CYNTHIA: I think what they did is bullshit. I promise you. I didn't know. I found out the same time as you guys . . . look . . . I'm in there fighting for us.

TRACEY: Us? You promised!!!

CYNTHIA: . . . If I'd known they were gonna ship out half of the machines, I woulda told you. But I didn't know until I got the call from Wilson.

TRACEY: Then why have you been avoiding us?

JASON: Yeah!

CYNTHIA: I'm not avoiding you! I'm working. And for your information, I'm the only supervisor who's even bothered to give you real face time.

TRACEY: Good for you, but what are we gonna do?! Huh?

CYNTHIA: I'm trying to get answers same as you. I just left the meeting . . .

JESSIE: What meeting?

CYNTHIA: I'm not even supposed to be talking to you guys.

TRACEY: Did they send you here?

CYNTHIA: Don't be an idiot, I'm off the clock, I'd lose my job if they knew I was here talking about this.

TRACEY: But I don't understand what you're telling us.

CYNTHIA: Okay, you're not going to like it, but they're going to use this opportunity to renegotiate your contracts.

TRACEY: What? Since when?   JESSIE: I fucking knew it.

CYNTHIA: And word is they're gonna push for real concessions, and they're prepared to fight.

JASON: Fuck that.

TRACEY: So are we. You tell   CHRIS: Nah.
'em no, they can't do that.

TRACEY: We're not afraid to strike.

CHRIS: Hell no!   JASON: Fuck yeah.

TRACEY: What do they want? Wasn't it enough that they
    shipped out the machines? And they better not ask us to
    work longer shifts.

CHRIS: Fuck that shit. I can't.   TRACEY: We're not mules.
    No!   We can't . . .

JESSIE: No way.   JASON: No fucking way.

CYNTHIA: I've told 'em there'd be blowback. I've been up three
    nights thinking about this. About you guys. But, I'm gonna
    be straight with you. They're eyeing jobs and some of you
    are making a lot of money.

TRACEY: What are you   CYNTHIA: You've been at
    making?   Olstead's a long time and
                                   they don't want to carry
                                   the burden anymore.

(Collective response.)

JESSIE: Oh, now we're the burden?

JASON: We're the fucking   CHRIS: Woah! Woah!
    burden?

CYNTHIA: With this NAFTA bullshit they can move the whole
    factory to Mexico tomorrow morning, and a woman like
    you will stand for sixteen hours and be happy making a
    fraction of what they're paying you.
TRACEY: Well, they can't do it.
JESSIE: Why now?

JASON: The union won't stand for it.

CHRIS: Lester's on it.

(Collective response.)

CYNTHIA: Guess what, the union don't got a lot to say about it.

JESSIE: What?   CHRIS: How's that possible?

CYNTHIA: Those machines are gone. They're not coming back.

JESSIE: Where are they?   CHRIS: That is fucked up.

(Collective response.)

CYNTHIA: But, if we do this right we can protect the rest of your jobs. That's the point. None of us wanna go anywhere. But be real, you think you're alone? Look at what went down at Clemmons. The union took a hard line, and look what happened to them. You wanna join those folks on unemployment, be my guest. But, listen—

TRACEY: C'mon.   JESSIE: I don't understand why
                                         this is happening!

CYNTHIA: I'm trying—

JESSIE: We work hard, our   JASON: If they got a problem,
        plant is making money.   why won't they be direct!

CHRIS: Let her speak. Let her speak. Ma, are they trying to squeeze us out?

CYNTHIA: You saw how easy it was for them to sneak in and break down those machines while all of us were at home sleeping.

JESSIE: // Where are the machines?

CYNTHIA: I guarantee you   CHRIS: Come the fuck on, man.
they're in Mexico.

CYNTHIA: Management is saying that it's too expensive for them
to operate here. I—

JASON: Why don't they take a pay cut if they wanna save their
precious plant?

CHRIS: Exactly!

CYNTHIA: Because they won't, and you know their solution, if
you don't meet them halfway, they'll pick up and run. That
way they won't even have to see your bodies as they flee.

JASON: That's bullshit.

CYNTHIA: I'm telling you what's going on. Right now, I don't
want this fucking job, but if I walk away, then you got
nobody. I may not have a lot of say, but I'm on your side.

TRACEY: Then act like it. You're making the same sorry excuses
that they do. We're friends!

CYNTHIA: . . . I am doing everything I can, babe. And I don't
know what more you want me to do?

TRACEY: Fight for us!

JASON: Yeah!

CYNTHIA: You think it's that easy?

TRACEY: All of us are on that line. Be straight!

CYNTHIA: . . .

CHRIS: Ma?!

TRACEY: Cynthia!

JESSIE: Just tell us the goddamn truth!

CHRIS: Step off and listen.

CYNTHIA: It ain't gonna be easy. I can tell you how it's gonna
play out. They're gonna ask for everyone to take a pay cut
to save jobs. Sixty percent.

TRACEY: What?

CHRIS: Sixty fucking percent?   JESSIE: Sixty?!

JASON: What the hell?

CYNTHIA: They're gonna ask for concessions on your benefits package next. I'm being straight. No bullshit. They're gonna ask you for more hours. They will give you a little bit of room for negotiation, and then they'll wait until your breaking point, at which time you'll be convinced that you've had a small victory.

TRACEY: What are you talking about?

CYNTHIA: Ask Lester, he's the union rep. He's been talking to them.

(Tracey fights back tears. Jason comforts her.)

JASON: They can't do this!

CHRIS: No!

JASON: And if we say no?

CHRIS: Yeah!

CYNTHIA: You're dealing with vipers. The game's changed! They'll lock you out. And once they get you out, they're not gonna let you back in.

TRACEY: Well, fuck you! Fuck them! I ain't going down without a fight. You can tell those bastards I will burn this factory down before I let them take my life.

JASON: Fuck yeah!

CHRIS: Word.

(A chorus of discontent.)

CYNTHIA: Now you know. The vote's coming! Decide!

(Silence.)

SCENE 3

August 4, 2000

Outside it's 80°F. Partly cloudy and pleasant.
In the news: Republican presidential candidate George W. Bush begins a post-convention train blitz across the Midwest.
Bar. Cynthia sits alone at a table. Stan pours her a drink.

CYNTHIA: On a cruise, Panama Canal. That's where I'd like to be right now. Poolside, piña colada in my hand. High and happy.

STAN: A nice breeze blowing off the water. Not a bad way to spend your birthday.

You all right? Hot in here? You want me to crank the air?

CYNTHIA: Nah, I'm okay.

(Cynthia looks around.)

I was kinda hoping they'd show up. It's the one thing we always do together.

STAN: Can you blame 'em?

CYNTHIA: Like I had a choice.

STAN: I'm just saying.

CYNTHIA: C'mon, Don't gimme that look.

STAN: Well, it can't be easy.

CYNTHIA: It isn't . . . You know what's crazy, when I started at the plant it felt like I was invited into an exclusive club. Not many of us folks worked there. Not us. So, when I put on my jacket, I knew I'd accomplished something. I was set. And when I got my union card, you couldn't tell me anything. Sometimes when I was shopping I would let it slip out of my wallet onto the counter just so folks could see it. I was that proud of it.

STAN: I remember the feeling.

(Cynthia smiles.)

CYNTHIA: Right. No one in my family ever made it beyond the floor.

STAN: // Yup . . .

CYNTHIA: And, I wanted this job so bad. Ever since I stepped into the plant, and saw how the white hats left work in clothes as clean as when they walked in. They seemed untouchable.

STAN: How are you holding up?

CYNTHIA: Shit. I locked out my friends, Stan. I explained, I fought, I begged. But those cowards upstairs still had me tape a note to the door telling 'em they weren't welcome. Ninety-five degrees. I'm standing in the door watching some irritable fat guy change the locks. Shut outta the plant. And you know what? I wonder if they gave me this job on purpose. Pin a target on me so they can stay in their air-conditioned offices. Do you know what it feels like, to say to the people you've worked with for years that they're not welcome anymore? I haven't slept in . . . in over a week.

STAN: Well, you're not alone.

CYNTHIA: I'm scared, Stan. I got a mortgage to meet, car payments, and Brucie, you've seen what being outta work has done to him. I'm not going down that way, I've worked too hard. Am I wrong?

STAN: Jesus.

CYNTHIA: I know. I know. But what could I have done? You tell me! The plant offered them a deal. The union voted it down. Not me!

STAN: What do you want me to say, sweetheart? Those are my friends.

CYNTHIA: Our friends.

STAN: Then imagine how they feel. Some folks wouldn't even want me to pour you a drink.

CYNTHIA: I've lived half my life on that floor. My son was practically born in that place. So don't get sanctimonious with me.

STAN: Okay, I'll keep out of it, but you know people will say what they say.

CYNTHIA: I thought they'd take the damn deal. You think I'm happy about this? I locked out my own son. My own son. I saw the hurt on his face. But you wanna know the truth, and this is the truth, maybe it's for the best, right? It'll finally get him out of this sinkhole.

(Cynthia doesn't finish her thought, but she's thinking it's all too hard. Stan senses this, and pours Cynthia another drink.)

STAN: It ain't your fault things shook out the way they did. I've spoken to a half dozen guys in your position. My cousin's over at Clemmons, they laid off four hundred people. Just like that, one day life is good, the next you're treading water. Clemmons! That's not supposed to happen to folks like us, but I'm pouring a lotta drinks these days. Business is good. You ain't the only one.

CYNTHIA: What the hell is going on, Stan?

STAN: Don't know. Don't get it. But, I watch these politicians talking bullshit and I get no sense that they even know what's going on beyond the windshield of their cars as they speed past. But, I decided a month ago that I'm not voting, cuz no matter what lever I pull it will lead to disappointment.

CYNTHIA *(Emotionally)*: Amen. You remember about seven months ago? Remember when Freddy Brunner burned down his house?

STAN: Of course.

CYNTHIA: We thought he was crazy.

STAN: Yeah.

CYNTHIA: Was he?

(Tracey and Jessie enter. They stop short upon seeing Cynthia. The tension is palpable.)

TRACEY *(Under her breath)*: Fucking traitor.

CYNTHIA: What did you say?

TRACEY: I said you fucking traitor.

JESSIE: How does it feel to shit on your friends?

(Cynthia stands up.)

CYNTHIA *(To Stan)*: I'm gonna go.

TRACEY: That's right. Walk away.

CYNTHIA: I'm not walking away, I'm leaving. There's a difference, don't get it confused. You know, you coulda taken the deal.

TRACEY: What deal?! I'd rather get locked out, and take handouts from the union than let go of everything I worked for. That's the truth.

JESSIE: What you did wasn't right!

TRACEY: They didn't even give us a fucking choice! After all of those years.

CYNTHIA: I just delivered the news, babe. I didn't make the policy.

JESSIE *(Shouts)*: You're supposed to be on our side!

CYNTHIA *(Shouts back)*: I am!

TRACEY: Do you know what it felt like to walk up to that plant, and be told after all them years I can't go in? I can't even go into my locker and get my stuff. I have photos of my husband in there. I have my grandfather's toolbox.

CYNTHIA: I'll get it for you, babe.

TRACEY: I don't want you to touch anything in that locker! They didn't even have the decency to let us clear out with dignity. A note taped to the door, what is that? And then to see you just standing there. I thought I was gonna lose my shit.

CYNTHIA: I tried to warn you. I hated it.

TRACEY: I looked for your eyes. Just gimme something, Cynth. A little look, to let me know it's okay, but you wouldn't even fucking look at me.

CYNTHIA: I'm in a tough-ass position, babe. I got enough attitude from folks to give me a heart attack. I'm trying to hold things together as best as I can.

TRACEY: What the fuck am I supposed to do? Huh? You coulda called me. Given me a heads-up. I mean come on. What am I supposed to do? Who's gonna hire me?

CYNTHIA: I know it hurts, babe. Take the deal.

TRACEY: NO! You hear yourself?

JESSIE: Can I have a beer, Stan?

STAN: Sure.

TRACEY: The other day, I walked over to the union office. Do you know what they offered me? A bag of groceries and some vouchers to the supermarket. They asked us to hold out, they're gonna help. Yeah, pay my fucking bills, that's how you can help. But, you know how many people were there for handouts? I looked for your eyes. Gimme something, Cynth. It was fucking humiliating.

CYNTHIA: Look, I'm sorry.

TRACEY: What am I supposed to do with that? Huh? What do you want me to do with that? You know what? This is my first time outta my house in one solid week. Do you know what it's like to get up and have no place to go? I ain't had the feeling ever. I'm a worker. I have worked since I could count money. That's me. And I'm thinking I'm not gonna go out, you know why? Because I don't wanna spend money, because when my unemployment runs out I'll have nothing. So, I don't go anywhere. And if Jessie hadn't called me, I'd still be sitting on my couch feeling sorry for myself, picking at my fucking cuticles. Why'd you come in here? Huh? What do you want?

CYNTHIA: It's my birthday. And this is where we've always celebrated.

(A moment. Tracey lights a cigarette.)

TRACEY: Do you remember that time we went to Atlantic City for your twenty-fifth?

CYNTHIA: Yeah, it was before Hank got sick.

TRACEY: The boys, Jason and Chris, were little. It was the four of us. You, Brucie, me and Hank. We splurged, got a suite.

CYNTHIA: Of course I remember . . . It was for the fight. Larry Holmes.

TRACEY: That's right. Hank had a friend, a high roller, and after the fight he invited us to one of those back-room clubs, you know very fancy. Champagne, buffet, seafood fountain, everything, really classy stuff.

CYNTHIA: Why are you bringing this up, Tracey?

TRACEY: Brucie was at the craps table rolling like a pro. Drenched in luck. It was just dripping off of him. The chips were leaping into his hands. And if I recall, he was also looking sorta fine that evening.

CYNTHIA: Yes, he was.

TRACEY: And then this chick.

CYNTHIA: C'mon, stop—

TRACEY: Yes. This chick. Legs, ass, boobs, weave. She was giving a full-service vibe, "walks" up and settles in next to Brucie—

JESSIE: "Settles"?

TRACEY: Her breasts were enormous, epic. Her dress, barely visible. I'm not a lesbian, but I couldn't take my eyes off of her boobs.

CYNTHIA: Why are you telling this story?

TRACEY: This chick was in heat, and she ever so gently places her hand on Brucie's shoulder, like this. I look over at Cynthia—

CYNTHIA: Don't—

TRACEY: And—

CYNTHIA: No—

TRACEY: She—

CYNTHIA: Lord, help me—

TRACEY: Is wearing the look: Stone Age. Prehistoric. T-rex. And I know what it means, Brucie knows what it means, but this bitch doesn't. Boobs leans over and whispers something into Brucie's ear. That's it. You just grab this chick's tits, and dig your fingernails in as hard as you can.

CYNTHIA: Yes, I did.

STAN: Whoa.

CYNTHIA: I'd had a couple tequilas. I wanted to deflate those fake tits. Puncture them with my fingernails.

TRACEY: Next thing I know, Cynthia's on the floor rolling around. Two grown women. It was sick. You put up a fight like a pro wrestler.

STAN: Jesus. Atlantic City. That's why I avoid it.

TRACEY: But, I remember thinking: that's my friend. She's tough as hell. Don't mess with her. She'll fight for what she loves, even if it means getting scrappy and looking ugly. That's my friend, and I miss the Cynthia who understood that.

CYNTHIA: What do you want from me, Tracey?

TRACEY: Walk out with us.

JESSIE: Walk with us. C'mon.

CYNTHIA: I can't.

JESSIE: C'mon.

CYNTHIA: I've stood on that line, same line since I was nineteen. I've taken orders from idiots who were dangerous, or even worse, racist. But I stood on line, patiently waiting for a break. I don't think you get it, but if I walk away, I'm giving up more than a job, I'm giving up all that time I spent standing on line waiting for one damn opportunity.

TRACEY: You want us to feel sorry for you?

CYNTHIA: . . . I didn't expect you to understand, babe. You don't know what it's been like to walk in my shoes. I've absorbed a lotta shit over the years, but I worked hard to get off that floor. Call me selfish, I don't care, call me whatever you need to call me, but remember, one of us has to be left standing to fight.

SCENE 4

September 28, 2000

Outside it's 63°F.

In the news: First Lady Hillary Rodham Clinton posts strong polling numbers in her New York Senate race against Rick Lazio. Americans Venus and Serena Williams win a gold medal in women's doubles tennis at the Sydney Summer Olympics. Three Mexican migrant farmworkers are killed when their car crashes into trees in Reading.

Bar. Brucie sits at a table, Stan is at the bar. Brucie is slightly disheveled, strung out. Chris and Jason stumbled in, all energy.

JASON: I don't wanna hear it. I don't care what anybody has to say, rhythmic gymnastics is not a sport!

CHRIS: You try catching a ball with your toes, and then tell me it's not a sport.

STAN: Chris.

(Stan gestures to Brucie slumped at the table.)

CHRIS *(Relieved)*: Jesus. Look atcha. Where've you been? I mean, I've been calling everyone. Goddamnit, where've you been?

BRUCIE: Chill. I'm here. Whassup?

CHRIS: Yo, J. Order me a beer.

JASON: Okay. *(Concern)* What's up, Brucie? You all right?

BRUCIE: Why wouldn't I be all right?

CHRIS: // Shit.

BRUCIE: You guys hanging tough?

JASON: You know. Miss the grind. Feeling the pinch. But Lester says it'll all work out.

BRUCIE: I've heard that before.

(Jason moves toward Brucie.)

JASON: Yo, everyone's been—

BRUCIE: I'm fine. Take a step back.

JASON: All right. All right.

(Jason moves to the bar.)

CHRIS: You can't do that. Disappear? Look at me. Where've you been?

BRUCIE: Around.

CHRIS: Mom won't say it, but she's worried as hell.

BRUCIE: Well, she has a damn funny way of showing it.

CHRIS: Nobody's seen you in a month. What's going on? What the hell? You stopped walking the line?

BRUCIE: . . . Yeah.

CHRIS: Dad! I'm talking to you! Where've you been?!!

BRUCIE: Um, crashing at your Uncle Cliff's crib, for now.

CHRIS: You need to pull yourself together! This bullshit's got to stop.

BRUCIE: I'm trying. Hey, don't give me that look. I'm trying. Okay?

CHRIS: . . .

BRUCIE: I'm *trying*.

CHRIS: You high?

BRUCIE: I'm a grown-ass man, I don't gots to report to nobody. Especially you, boy! So step off.

CHRIS: That's all you got for me? Then go be a zombie, I don't give a shit.

(Chris goes to sit at the bar.)

JASON: Leave it.

(A moment.)

BRUCIE: C'mon. Chris. I didn't come down here for this. C'mon.

CHRIS: What's going on with you? Earl and Saunders, both of 'em called me.

BRUCIE: I dunno. Can I tell you something that happened a couple of weeks ago?

CHRIS: You know what, I don't wanna // hear your bullshit—

BRUCIE: Chris . . . please! Chris!

(Chris walks over to Brucie.)

CHRIS: What?

BRUCIE: I was doing my rotation on the line, same as always. And it began to rain, all at once a downpour, folks fled, but I . . . I just stood there . . . couldn't move. I got soaked through to my skin. I still couldn't move. And . . . and finally someone pulled me into the tent to get dry, but my whole body was shaking, wouldn't stop. It was scary. And I hadn't had that feeling of being outta control since my mother died.

CHRIS: You okay? Don't let 'em do this to you.

BRUCIE: . . .

CHRIS: You hear me?

BRUCIE: Yeah. Yeah. I'm okay. Will you buy me a drink?

CHRIS: . . . Sure.

BRUCIE: Thank you. Thank you.

(Chris crosses to the bar. Stan pours a beer.)

And you . . . you guys awright?

CHRIS: It's been rough. Man, they're testing us. Folks are getting real hot.

JASON: Tell me about it!

CHRIS: I see those dudes heading into the plant and I wanna smack 'em—

JASON *(Clenching his fist)*: Fucking pricks!

BRUCIE: I hear that. But whassup? You start school?

CHRIS: Nah, I didn't enroll this semester.

BRUCIE: Why? What's your mom think about that?

CHRIS: Things have been a little strained between us. So—

BRUCIE: You need to tell her.

CHRIS: Why? I know what she's gonna say. But, you feel me, right?

BRUCIE: . . .

CHRIS: Right? And with the shit that's going down I didn't make tuition. Things are tight. I was counting on those double shifts this summer.

BRUCIE: Look, Chris, I can't help you // I'm—

CHRIS: I'm not looking for your help. Okay? My head's not in it right now.

BRUCIE: You need to get your head in it. I've been out here, and shit's real. You sure this is a good idea?

CHRIS: It's what it is! And you're the one that's always saying—

BRUCIE: Never mind // what—

CHRIS: You taught me how to throw a rock. I remember the first time you walked the line.

BRUCIE: Yeah, we were out almost two months. What about it?

CHRIS: There was this one night you had a big meeting at the house.

BRUCIE: // Yeah—

CHRIS: Like ten–fifteen guys. It was loud, like a street brawl. I was hiding in the doorway, I had no idea what you guys were talking about, but it felt like it was gonna get ugly—

BRUCIE: It was when Bobby Holden lost his hand in the mill.

CHRIS: And you were all shouting about how you were gonna vote if they didn't meet your demands.

BRUCIE: That's right.

CHRIS: And suddenly you stood up, and for like a second you looked like another man, bigger, like a Transformer, and when you spoke everyone got real calm and began nodding. You said, um . . . "We . . . we will not continue to bare our backs for them to strike us down."

BRUCIE: Is that really what I said?

CHRIS: Or something like that. I dunno. But, I remember the fire in your voice and how it made me feel. And after school, me and my friends rode our bikes to the mill and watched you guys picketing. You looked like warriors, arms linked, standing together.

BRUCIE: Fuckin' Bobby Holden—

CHRIS: And you know, yesterday as I was walking the line, and listening to Lester tell us about what we'd have to sacrifice to keep the plant running, all I could think about was your words that evening. You! What it means to stand strong.

BRUCIE: It's tough for me to say, I'm union to the end, but this don't have to be your fight. // You—

CHRIS: But it is. I'm not gonna be a punk-ass bitch! That's what they want.

JASON: That's right!

CHRIS: I don't care what anybody gots to say, we're gonna stand together. And they're not gonna break us!

JASON: Hell, yes!

BRUCIE: You think they give a damn about your black ass?! Let me tell you something, they don't even see you!

CHRIS: I'm gonna make 'em see me.

BRUCIE: You think so?! After that storm hits, and all the dust clears, who's gonna pick you up? Huh?

CHRIS: . . .

BRUCIE: You got options that I didn't. School always scared me, that's the honest-to-God truth. That's all I'm saying.

(A moment.)

You really wanna know where I been?

CHRIS: . . . No.

BRUCIE: I didn't think so. Don't back away from what you want. That line is gonna thin out, and then what? That's what I'm trying to figure out—and then what?!

SCENE 5

October 26, 2000

Outside it's 72°F.

In the news: After yet another gun incident at a school, Attorney General Janet Reno reassures the public that "American schools are safe places." 200 people camp overnight at a Reading electronics superstore hoping to be the first to buy the $350 Sony PlayStation 2.

Bar. Television screen. Jessie sits slumped at a table. Stan is checking inventory.

Oscar enters. A moment.

STAN: So, when were you gonna tell me?

OSCAR: What?

STAN: . . . You crossed the line.

OSCAR: Who told you?

STAN: Nelson.

OSCAR: They were hiring part-time temps to replace some of the locked-out workers. I can pick up a couple of hours in the mornings, and maybe get a full shift.

STAN: Be careful.

OSCAR: Why?

STAN: Why?! Emotions are running high. That's why.

OSCAR: Yeah, well, they're offering eleven dollars an hour.

STAN: I know. Looks good from where you're standing, but that eleven dollars is gonna come outta the pockets of a lot of good people. And they ain't gonna like it.

OSCAR: Well, I'm sorry about that. But it ain't my problem. I been trying to get into that shop for two years. And each time I asked any of 'em, I get nothing but pushback. So now, I'm willing to be a little flexible and they ain't.

STAN: You want my opinion?

OSCAR: Do I have a choice?

STAN: Don't do it.

OSCAR: That's your opinion. You gonna give me a raise? Huh?

STAN: It's not up to me, it's Howard's call. I just put the money in the till, I ain't responsible for taking it out. But, let me ask him.

OSCAR: They're offering me three dollars more per hour than I make here. Three dollars. What they're offering is better than anything I've touched since I got outta high school. So yo, I ain't afraid to cross the line. Let 'em puff up their chest, but it don't scare me no more than walking through my 'hood. I know rough. I ain't afraid to roll in the dirt.

STAN: Fine, tough guy. But, trust me you're gonna make some real enemies. Couple of folks you know.

OSCAR: They ain't my friends. They don't come into my house and water my plants.

STAN: Okay. But for the record, I think it's seriously fucked up. Six months, watch, they're gonna get another set of guys like you who'll cross the line, and guess what? They'll offer them ten dollars. Watch. Then you'll be outta a job, wanting someone to stand by you. But ain't nobody gonna do it. And, let me tell you something. My ol' man—

OSCAR: Yeah, yeah—

STAN: Don't you "yeah, yeah" me. My dad put forty-two years into building that plant, those benefits, those wages, that vacation time you're so hungry for, guess what? He fought for 'em when the going wasn't so great. That's right. And you think you're gonna walk in and tear it all down in a day. There are folks out there that won't go down easy.

OSCAR: Why are you coming at me that way? I'm not disrespectin' you. I'm just trying to get paid, that's all. For three years I've been carrying nothing but crates. I've got twenty-dollar bills taped to my wall, and a drawer full of motivational tapes. Got a jar of buena suerte from the botanica, and a candle that I keep lit 24/7. I keep asking for some good fortune. That's it. A little bit of money. That's it. My father, he swept up the floor in a factory like Olstead's— those fuckas wouldn't even give him a union card. But he woke up every morning at four A.M. because he wanted a job in the steel factory, it was the American way, so he swept fucking floors thinking, "One day they'll let me in." I know how he feels, people come in here every day. They brush by me without seeing me. No: "Hello, Oscar." If they don't see me, I don't need to see them.

STAN: I hear ya. But, c'mon, really? Look elsewhere, not Olstead's. You don't wanna do this.

OSCAR: You know what I don't wanna do? This.

(Oscar makes a show of putting on his apron. He then lifts and carries a crate of beers into the back.
Tracey stumbles in, untidy. She goes to the end of the bar.)

TRACEY: Hey, Stan.

STAN: Look who it is. I been holding a spot, you want me to put you down for fifty dollars for the Series' pool?

TRACEY: Nah. Not this time.

STAN: You sure? You won two years ago.

TRACEY: Not this time. Um, can I have a double vodka on the rocks?

(Stan pours a drink.)

STAN: You keeping yourself busy?

TRACEY: Trying. Been walking the line in the mornings. Working the phones in the afternoon. Nothing yet. Union's offering money for folks to go back to school, but I never liked school, so I'm taking what little support they give until I can find something to pay the bills.

STAN: Almost three months. Fuck.

TRACEY: Who woulda thought.

STAN: I still think the way everything went down—

TRACEY: Don't. Stop it. Everyone is treating us like we lost a limb. I'm fine. And the good news is, my back pain is gone.

STAN: Glad to hear it.

TRACEY: Thanks. Put my drink on the tab.

STAN: I can't. Gotta run your card.

TRACEY: Since when?

STAN: Howard. That's what he wants.

TRACEY: Stan! C'mon.

STAN: Sorry.

TRACEY: I don't have a credit card.

STAN: Sorry. Too many folks not paying. Howard's cracking down.

TRACEY: Stan! It's me.

STAN: Can't.

TRACEY *(Pointing to Jessie)*: How's she paying?

STAN: She pays.

TRACEY: She's crashing with her sister, betcha she goes into her purse at night.

(Tracey downs the drink. Then digs into her pocket. She makes a show of counting out loose change on the bar.)

STAN: Oh, for God's sake. Really?

TRACEY: You changed the rules, not me.

(Tracey continues to make a show of counting her coins.)

Fucking Howard. Jesus, I just came down here to get outta the house to relax.

STAN: Awright, awright. You're so dramatic. Today it's on me, but now you know.

TRACEY: I know. I know. God, I know, already. Thank you. I love you.

STAN: Do you?

TRACEY: Not going there.

STAN: I'm just saying. Life might be a little easier if you did.

TRACEY: I'm not sure whether you're being really romantic or a little bit sleazy.

STAN: Whatever turns you on. You know where I stand.

(Oscar reenters and looks at Tracey, sheepishly.)

TRACEY: Well, I ain't that desperate. *(To Oscar)* What are you looking at?

OSCAR: Is that how you say hello?

TRACEY: Yeah, to a fuck-face scab like you. You're a piece of shit.

STAN: Hey, c'mon. None of that.

OSCAR: If you wasn't a woman I'd slap you in your mouth. You're lucky I was raised good.

TRACEY: Well, I wasn't.   STAN: Hey, hey hey!

(Tracey charges toward Oscar. Stan intercepts, and holds her back. Oscar laughs.)

OSCAR: What are you gonna do?

STAN: Oscar! Take a break.

TRACEY: Let's see if you talk // to me that way when my son is here.

OSCAR: I have no problem with you. This ain't personal.

TRACEY: You better believe it's personal . . . for me.

SCENE 6

November 3, 2000

Outside it's 66°F.
   In the news: It's four days before the U.S. election and George Bush and Al Gore are running neck and neck in the polls. The Mayor of Reading proposes a budget to increase earned income tax.
   Bar. Chris and Jason burst in, adrenaline pumping. Jessie sits at a table, shit-faced but content.

CHRIS: They better not come at me again! // Cuz—
JASON: I'm ready! I'm ready for whatever they got!
STAN: What the hell's going on?
JASON *(Amped up)*: Aw, some of the guys got into a scrape with the scabs. McManus got cut, he's gonna need ten stitches on the side of his face.
STAN: Yeah?

JASON: Some of the guys feel we shouldn't make it so easy to cross the line.

STAN: Don't like the sound of that.

CHRIS: Some shit, huh?

STAN: Seen it before. It's not gonna help your cause.

(Jason sneaks a drink from a small bottle of whiskey tucked in his pocket.)

CHRIS: Same shit, nobody's budging. The workers coming in ain't feeling so temporary.

STAN: Tough. Whatcha gonna do?

JASON: Who the fuck knows? There's a few guys, Stubbs, Godski, talking about taking the deal, but I don't know, seems like a big waste of time if we give in now. They'll break us, and there's no going back. I figure I can hold out another three months. Push comes to shove, I'll sell the bike. But me, honestly, I think we teach some of those guys a lesson, what do you think?

STAN: Hell, why are you asking me? I dunno. You're young, I mean there are a lotta things you could do. Maybe it's time to move on, this place ain't what it used to be.

JASON: And go where?

STAN: Anywhere. Sometimes I think we forget that we're meant to pick up and go when the well runs dry. Our ancestors knew that. You stay put for too long, you get weighed down by things, things you don't need. It's true. Then your life becomes this pathetic accumulation of stuff. Emotional and physical junk. You gotta ask yourself what you're hanging on to, huh? I knew your dad, he was a good enough guy, but that place took him young. Sure he made decent money, but jacking's hard—

CHRIS: Word.

JASON: Well, if things get too real, I got a buddy who works on a rig in the Gulf, says he can get me something in the spring.

STAN: Yeah? I hear you can make like a grand a week. Work half the year, and then do whatever.

JASON: Yeah. Just gotta get the card, and get down there.

STAN: Why the hell not? Me, if I was thirty years younger, I'd already be down there. Nothing but mildew lingering in these cracks. This place is for shit. Sure, it used to be something. But nostalgia's a disease, I'm not gonna be one of those guys that surrenders to it. What do you get?

CHRIS: I don't wanna think about it. My jaw's tired of the damn chatter. Just wanna get drunk, smoke a blunt and chill for a little while.

JASON: That's an excellent plan.

CHRIS: You know . . . I see my dad and—

STAN: He's going through a rough patch.

CHRIS: That's very polite. Not me, I'll probably ride out unemployment, maybe pick up some heavy lifting, day stuff, then start college next September. The union's offering some financial aid.

JASON: I can tell ya what they're gonna say: "Fuck you, fuck you and—"

(Jason playfully jumps on Chris's back.)

CHRIS AND JASON: "Fuck you!"

STAN: All right, all right. Break it up before it gets too kinky.

CHRIS: Whatcha got on tap?

STAN: The usual! C'mon, why do ya gotta ask me that every single time?

CHRIS: Keep hoping for a surprise.

STAN: You're in the fucking wrong town for that. *(Laughs)* How's your girl? I haven't seen her around.

CHRIS: It didn't work out.

JASON: She couldn't fit his big dick in her mouth.

CHRIS: Shut up!

JASON: She was—

CHRIS: Shut up!

JASON: She—

CHRIS: Was sweating me.

STAN: Yeah? How long wuz you together?

CHRIS: Just under a year. She was pushing for more. But, I wasn't feeling it, whatever holds people together, that thing. I didn't feel it. So I guess, it's for the best. No?

STAN: Good for you.

CHRIS: I told my girl that things were gonna be tight for a little while. And she's all like, "What does that mean for us?" I break it down. It's gonna get real. And she's like, "Well, you need to find another job, playa." I tell her that's what I'm trying to do. But she got that old-school mentality, she wants what she wants in the moment, and can't be thinking about tomorrow. Yo, she was too much work for a man outta work. She was plenty happy when I was a paycheck, numbers and pretty things, but the minute I ask her to borrow twenty dollars to put a little gas in the car she treats me like I've broken into her crib. What's that about?

STAN: I remain unattached for those very reasons.

CHRIS: Now is the moment. You're right, Stan. Maybe we should move on. We can complain until kingdom come. Bla, bla, bla. That shit gets old real fast. I'm out there on the picket lines every morning. I shout "fuck you" at a bunch of pathetic hungry guys. I feel good and superior about it all, for like five minutes, and then reality hits. They're inside. And then I think about my pops. Who wants that shit?

JASON: Yo, if I was—

CHRIS: Hey, yo, shut up, man! Don't say nothing, Jason, because I swear I will punch you out. And just let me finish! Okay? I used to worry about what people would think if I didn't want to work in the factory. Now they got us fighting for scraps. But, Stan said it, the writing's on the wall, and we're still out here pretending like we can't read.

JASON: Women cost money. All the shit they want these days, it's too much. You gotta sew your pockets shut.

CHRIS: Wow, really, that's your takeaway from what I just said?

(Jessie, suddenly:)

JESSIE: No. You're a cheap-ass bastard.
CHRIS: Go to rehab!
JASON: But, seriously—

(Tracey comes out of the bathroom.)

TRACEY: Why don't you ever have paper towels?
STAN: Doing our little bit for the environment.
TRACEY: Hey Jason, buy your mom a drink.

(Tracey drapes herself around Jason's shoulders and gives him a kiss.)

JASON: Really? C'mon. That means I won't be able to have another one.
TRACEY: Poor baby, what ever happened to the notion of sacrifice?
STAN: Jason, c'mon.
CHRIS: I got you, Mrs. T.
TRACEY: Is it your mother's money?
CHRIS: . . . No.
TRACEY: Then okay. Stan. Pour!

(Jessie rouses.)

JESSIE: Hey, gimme one while the bottle's open.

(Stan pours Jessie and Tracey drinks.)

JASON: Jesus, Chris, you're making me look bad.
CHRIS: Don't have to try very hard.
TRACEY: Okay, I got a story for you guys—

JASON: Oh no.

TRACEY: Shut up, you gotta hear it, you guys know Ronnie Gol-molka, well he got caught—

(Oscar walks in. Tracey sees him and stops talking. It's too late for Oscar to retreat.)

OSCAR: Hey Stan.

STAN: Oscar.

OSCAR: I came to pick up the rest of my stuff. But, if now ain't such a good time . . . I thought . . .

(Jason and Chris stare down Oscar. Stan breaks the tension.)

STAN: It's in the back. You want me to get it?

OSCAR: Nah, I'll get it.

JESSIE *(Shouts)*: Fucking scab!

(Oscar goes to the back. Jason stands up.)

STAN: Don't!

JASON: Don't what?

STAN: You know what. Sit down.

JASON: That fucking spic.

STAN: Hey, hey, c'mon. None of that in here. Oscar's a good guy. Let him get his stuff, okay?

JASON: I don't give a fuck.

TRACEY: Amen. That piece of shit knows what he's doing. I don't care about his sorry story. So what he's got an apartment filled with seventeen relatives that gotta eat. I'm tired of their shit. I worked that line for over twenty years and he thinks he can push in.

STAN: Enough, c'mon. This is neutral territory.

JASON: She's got a point. I'll be damned if I'm gonna let that fucker walk over my toes. It ain't gonna happen.

CHRIS: J, sit the fuck down, you don't got a beef with him. Not here. He's just—

JASON: What?

CHRIS: Trying to make a dollar. Okay? The same as you or me.

JASON: Nah, it ain't the same. We got history here. Us! Me, you, him, her! What the fuck does he have, huh? A green card that gives him the right to shit on everything we worked for?

STAN: Why don't you take a walk around the block?

CHRIS: Yeah, let's go.

(Chris tries to pull Jason out. Jason wrenches himself away.)

JASON: Do you hear yourself? I'm the problem? I should sit the fuck down? No way.

CHRIS: Let it alone. Fuck 'em. Now, ain't the moment. That muthafucka ain't worth it. Okay?

TRACEY: Did you see the way he looked at you guys? He's eating your dinner, your steak and potatoes, your fucking dessert.

JESSIE: Yum! Yum!

(Jessie laughs.)

STAN: Shut up!

TRACEY: I'm not shutting up!

JESSIE: Tell 'em.

STAN *(To Jason)*: You heard, it ain't worth it. Why do you need trouble?

JASON: Just gonna set him straight. Simple talk.

STAN: Don't be an asshole.

JASON: I'm an asshole? What I done? Eleven dollars an hour? No thank you. They'll work us down to nothing if we let 'em. "Jacking ain't for softies!" But they know they can always find somebody willing to get their hands sweaty. And they're right. There will always be someone who'll step in, unless we say NO!

STAN: Look. Olstead is a prick. If he was here I wouldn't stop you. In fact I'd hold him down for you to give him a proper

SWEAT

101

beating, but Oscar . . . he's another story. He's gonna walk outta here, and you, you're gonna keep your mouth shut or I—

JASON: What?! All I'm saying is that he needs to understand the price of that dinner he's putting on his table.

STAN (*Shouts*): What the fuck do you want him to do? Huh? It ain't his fault. Talk to Olstead, his cronies. Fucking Wall Street. Oscar ain't getting rich off your misery.

CHRIS: Jason, he's right. He's hustling. We're all hustling.

JASON: Chris, what's wrong with you? He ain't with us otherwise he'd be walking the line. Am I the only one seeing this clearly?

TRACEY: No, you're not wrong. He's breaking the rules, not us!

STAN: Don't let her get into your head. She's drunk.

TRACEY: So what? It don't change the truth.

JESSIE: // That's for sure.

STAN: You can either sit back down or you can leave. I'm dead serious. But, you're not starting trouble in here. Not with Oscar!

JASON: Oh, I see how this is gonna be.

(*Stan slams a bat onto the bar.*)

STAN: SIT DOWN!

(*Jason reluctantly sits, the boy inside prevails.*)

CHRIS: Yo, let's finish up, and drive over to see what Gibney's up to.

JASON (*Moping*): Yeah, maybe.

CHRIS: Play some cards. Win some money off of him. Two drinks and he's sloppy and he'll open up his wallet.

JASON (*Smiling*): Yeah.

CHRIS: Hit up a club in Philly.

JASON: Sounds good.

CHRIS: Cool?

JASON: Cool. I'm all right. I was just, you know—

CHRIS: Okay—

JASON: Whatever. I'm fine.

TRACEY *(To Jason)*: That's the problem. We all just roll over, and offer up our assholes for anyone who wants to fuck us. We will be fucked. Chris, they fucked your father, and Jason, if your father was here, I'd tell you what he'd do, he'd—

(Jason balls up his fist.)

STAN *(To Tracey)*: Shut up!

JASON: Hey, watch your mouth. Don't talk to her that way.

(Oscar reenters with a backpack slung over his shoulder.)

STAN: Take care.

OSCAR: Thanks for everything.

STAN: And tell your ma, thank you for the aripa.

OSCAR: Arepas. Will do.

STAN: Don't be a stranger.

(They shake hands. Oscar heads for the door.)

TRACEY: Hey Jason, he's heading out to cash your check.

STAN: Oh shit.

(Before Oscar can get to the door Jason pops up and blocks his path. They stand face to face, eye to eye. A game of Chicken.)

OSCAR: Excuse me.

(Jason doesn't move.)

I said, excuse me.

(Jason still doesn't move. Oscar goes to walk around him. Again Jason blocks his path.)

STAN: Let him pass, Jason.

(Jason provokes Oscar.)

OSCAR: I don't have no problem with you.
JASON: Too late for that

(Chris stands up.)

CHRIS: Yo J, let's get up from outta here, okay?

(Stan moves from behind the bar.)

JASON: I can't. I don't know why, but I can't let him walk outta here.
STAN: Sure you can! Nobody here is gonna think any less of you.
OSCAR: Move!
JASON: Or?

(A stare-down. Jason shoves Oscar.
Stan intervenes, grabbing Jason's arm. Jason shoves him away violently. Stan loses his balance and tumbles to the ground. Oscar goes to aid Stan, but Jason grabs him first.)

JESSIE: Oh shit!

(A loud and untidy fight ensues. It tumbles across the bar. Oscar manages to hold his own against Jason. Oscar breaks free, and runs for the door.)

OSCAR: Fuck you!

(Jason grabs Oscar. They tussle. Tracey picks up a glass to throw. Chris grabs her. Then Jason grabs Oscar. The fight continues. Chris tries to break it up. Oscar head-butts Chris, bloodying his nose.)

Bitch!

JESSIE: Don't let him go.

(*Chris's anger has been ignited. He puts Oscar in a headlock and punches him several times in the stomach. Oscar drops to his knees.*)

CHRIS: Motherfucker!

(*Chris kicks him in the ribs. Oscar writhes in pain. Jason grabs the bat from the bar.*)

JASON: Hold him!

(*Chris grabs Oscar and yanks him to his feet. Tracey watches the battle, her face contorted with rage.*)

STAN: Let him go!

(*Stan manages to get to his feet, but it's too late. Jason hits Oscar in the stomach with the bat. Oscar crumples to the ground. Jason hits him again. As Jason winds up for another swing, Stan tries to intervene, but the bat hits him hard in the head. Stan falls back, hitting his head on the bar—blood. He slumps to the ground. Jessie gasps. Jason, and then Chris, recognizes the weight of what they've done. They flee.*)

TRACEY: Stan?!

TRANSITION

September 24, 2008

In the news: President Bush prepares to present a very dire warning to the American people. He will suggest that unless Congress approves a $700,000,000,000 bailout for Wall Street, and it is approved within a matter of only a few days, there will be ominous consequences for the entire U.S. economy and for millions of Americans.

SCENE 7

October 15, 2008

Outside it's 77°F.

    In the news: Baghdad and Washington have reached a final agreement on a pact requiring U.S. forces to withdraw from Iraq by 2012. U.S. stocks plunge 733 points, the second biggest point loss in history. John McCain and Barack Obama hold their final televised debate at Hofstra University in Hempstead, New York. Federal prosecutors convict a multimillion-dollar drug ring that converted several Reading houses into indoor marijuana farms.

    Evan stands over Chris, who is finishing describing his encounter with Jason.

EVAN: It's not a big place. You two were bound to run into each other sooner or later. I don't want this to be a problem.

CHRIS: I'd spent so much time being angry at Jason, but standing there I don't even know what I was feeling.

EVAN: That's okay. These things ain't simple. I had a 'banger who was up in here, hard as stone. He got out, made amends, crossed so many bridges he was practically walking on water. He found forgiveness to be the easier of his two paths.

CHRIS: Dunno about all of that. Shit, I remember when I sat down at the bar I knew I didn't want the same flat-ass beer that Stan always poured. I knew I was gonna drive down to Philly that evening and hit a club with some friends. And the next day, I had planned to go over to Albright. I was feeling free, like for the first time I had an option other than jacking and a hangover. And I coulda walked away, and today I'd // be—

EVAN: Don't.

CHRIS: I hate the way people be looking at me now. I feel like they can see what I done. I pray on it. I ask for forgiveness. But every morning I wake up with the same panic. All I see is a closed door, and when I finally get the courage to open it, it leads to yet another closed door.

(Evan shifts. He is now talking to Jason.)

EVAN: Maybe you two need to sit down and talk?

JASON: . . . Yeah. I hear you. Been thinking.

(Jason smiles.)

EVAN: That's new. Look, I know what you're avoiding, and man, I don't blame you, but—

JASON: I ain't thought about that day in the bar in a long time. Now I can't get away from it. Every place I walk in this city reminds me of that day, it's like the whole city was in that bar and got turned upside down in the same way I did.

EVAN: Got a call that you were fighting at the shelter. That true? Where are you sleeping these days?

JASON: My mom's place was too depressing, and a friend of mine gave me a tent and sleeping bag, so I've been camping in the woods with a couple of other guys. It's easy.

EVAN: I'm gonna need an address.

JASON: It don't cost me nothing. It's easier than playing musical beds at the shelter. Nobody calls me out.

EVAN: It's gonna get cold soon.

JASON: Well, I'll cross that bridge when I get there. Ever since I ran into Chris I haven't been able to focus. I'm trying to figure it out, you know? What happened. I just remember the fury. The blind fury. And I ain't been able to shake it. It's like a wool jacket that I wear all of the fucking time. Someone looks at me wrong, I wanna bash them in the face, and I don't know why.

EVAN: Man, you're not gonna like what I have to say. But I'm just gonna say it. Shame.

JASON: What?

EVAN: I've seen enough guys in your situation to know that over time it's . . . it's crippling. I'm not a therapist, I'm not the right dude to talk to about all of this. But what I do know, is that it's not a productive emotion. Most folks think it's the guilt or rage that destroys us in the end, but I know from experience that it's shame that eats us away until we disappear. You put in your time. But look here, we been talking, and we can keep talking—but whatcha gonna do about where you're at right now? You hear me?

(Light shift. We're back with Chris.)

JASON: Yeah.

CHRIS: Yeah, I hear you.

SCENE 8

October 18, 2008

Outside it's 58°F.

In the news: Thousands of Latin American immigrants are returning home as U.S. jobs dry up in the construction, landscaping and restaurant industries. Pennsylvania's Republican Party sues the community activist group ACORN, accusing the group of fostering voter registration fraud. The Philadelphia Phillies prepare to face off against the Tampa Bay Rays in the 2008 Major League Baseball World Series.

Bar. It has been refurbished, polished. Oscar, older and more mature, stands behind the bar. Chris enters and reluctantly sits at a table. A moment. Oscar contemplates whether to speak.

OSCAR: You want me to turn on the game?

CHRIS: Nah. You awright?

OSCAR: Yeah. I heard you guys got out.

(A moment.)

CHRIS: Oscar, I—
OSCAR: Didn't know you knew my name.
CHRIS: I—
OSCAR: Whatchu drinking?
CHRIS: . . . Whatcha got on tap?
OSCAR: It's this artisanal stuff. A guy, local, makes it.
CHRIS: You're joking.
OSCAR: Nah. It's good.
CHRIS: Um, okay.

(Oscar pours a beer.)

The place looks nice.
OSCAR: New crowd. We get a lot of college kids since the plant
    closed. I been trying to keep it up, you know—
CHRIS: Yeah. How's, um, Howard?
OSCAR: Retired. Moved to Phoenix. I'm the manager.
CHRIS: Really?
OSCAR: Yeah. Bartend on weekends.
CHRIS: That's real cool.
OSCAR: Thanks.
CHRIS: I . . .
OSCAR: Look. Whatever you gotta say—
CHRIS: Listen—

(Jason enters. Oscar's surprised, and grows a little on edge.)

OSCAR: Whoa, what's going on here?

(Jason stops short, panic, then turns to leave.)

CHRIS: Jason!
OSCAR: I don't want—
JASON: Yo, I can't do—

CHRIS: Don't walk outta here. I didn't think you'd come. We have—

(A moment. Jason contemplates whether or not to leave. Then Stan, severely crippled, enters. A traumatic brain injury. He moves with extreme difficulty; it is painful to watch. Finally:)

Hey Stan. Stan.

(Stan doesn't register their presence.)

OSCAR: He can't really hear good.
CHRIS: Jesus.

(Stan goes about wiping tables. They all watch. Stan drops his cloth. He struggles to get it. Jason runs over and picks it up.)

STAN *(Garbled)*: Thank . . . you.
JASON: It's nice that you take care of him.
OSCAR: That's how it oughta be.

(There's apology in their eyes, but Chris and Jason are unable to conjure words just yet. The four men, uneasy in their bodies, await the next moment in a fractured togetherness.
Blackout.)

END OF PLAY

LYNN NOTTAGE has been awarded the Pulitzer Prize for Drama twice (for *Sweat* and *Ruined*), the first woman ever to do so. Her plays have been produced in the U.S. and throughout the world. *Sweat* (Pulitzer Prize, Susan Smith Blackburn Prize) moved to Broadway after a sold-out run at The Public Theater in New York City. It premiered and was commissioned by Oregon Shakespeare Festival's American Revolutions History Cycle/Arena Stage. *By the Way, Meet Vera Stark* received the Lilly Award, and a Drama Desk nomination. *Ruined* received the Pulitzer Prize, an Obie Award, a Lucille Lortel Award, the New York Drama Critics' Circle Award, an AUDELCO Award, a Drama Desk Award, and an Outer Critics Circle Award. *Intimate Apparel* received the American Theatre Critics and New York Drama Critics' Circle Awards for Best Play. *Fabulation, or the Re-Education of Undine* received an Obie Award. Her other plays include *Crumbs from the Table of Joy*; *Las Meninas*; *Mud, River, Stone*; *Por'knockers*; and *POOF*. She is working with the composer Ricky Ian Gordon on the adaptation of *Intimate Apparel* into an opera (commissioned by The Metropolitan Opera and Lincoln Center Theater). She is also developing *This Is Reading*, a performance installation set to open at the Reading Railroad Station in Reading, Pennsylvania, in the summer of 2017.

She is the co-founder of the production company Market Road Films. Recent projects include *The Notorious Mr. Bout*, directed by Tony Gerber and Maxim Pozdorovkin (Premiere/

Sundance 2014); *First to Fall*, directed by Rachel Beth Anderson and Timothy Grucza (Premiere/IDFA).

She has developed original projects for HBO, Sidney Kimmel Entertainment, Showtime, This Is That, and Harpo. She is a writer/producer on the Netflix series *She's Gotta Have It*, directed by Spike Lee.

Nottage is the recipient of a PEN/Laura Pels Master American Dramatist Award; an Award of Merit Medal and a Literature Award from The Academy of Arts and Letters; a Provost Grant; a Doris Duke Artist Award; The Joyce Foundation Commission Project and Grant; the Madge Evans and Sidney Kingsley Award; a MacArthur "Genius Grant" Fellowship; a Steinberg Distinguished Playwright Award; a Nelson A. Rockefeller Award for Creativity; The Dramatists Guild Hull-Warriner Award; the inaugural Horton Foote Prize; the Helen Hayes Award; the Lee Reynolds Award; and the Jewish World Watch I Witness Award. Her other honors include the National Black Theatre Fest's August Wilson Playwriting Award, a Guggenheim Grant, the Lucille Lortel Fellowship, and a Visiting Research Fellowship at Princeton University.

She is a graduate of Brown University and the Yale School of Drama. She is also an associate professor in the Theatre Department at the Columbia School of the Arts. She is member of The Dramatists Guild and WGAE.

Theatre Communications Group would like to offer our special thanks to Paula Marie Black for her generous support of the publication of Sweat *by Lynn Nottage*

P AULA MARIE BLACK is a Drama Desk, Drama League, Tony Award, Olivier Award, and Helpmann Award–winning producer dedicating her efforts in theatre to women directors, playwrights, and all people who have not had a voice.

Women's Voices in the Art of Theatre is an endowment that Paula established in perpetuity at La Jolla Playhouse, benefitting women as directors, playwrights, and book writers of musicals.

TCG books sponsored by Paula include:

Annie Baker, *John*
Amy Herzog, *The Great God Pan* and *Belleville*
Lynn Nottage, *Sweat*
Suzan-Lori Parks, *The Book of Grace*
Paula Vogel, *Indecent*